Houghton Mifflin CALIFORNIA
Math Expressions

Volume 2

Developed by
The Children's Math Worlds
Research Project

PROJECT DIRECTOR AND AUTHOR
Dr. Karen C. Fuson

 This material is based upon work supported by the
National Science Foundation
under Grant Numbers
ESI-9816320, REC-9806020, and RED-935373.

Any opinions, findings, and conclusions or recommendations expressed in this material are those of the author and do not necessarily reflect the views of the National Science Foundation.

 HOUGHTON MIFFLIN   BOSTON

Teacher Reviewers

Kindergarten
Patricia Stroh Sugiyama
Wilmette, Illinois

Barbara Wahle
Evanston, Illinois

Grade 1
Sandra Budson
Newton, Massachusetts

Janet Pecci
Chicago, Illinois

Megan Rees
Chicago, Illinois

Grade 2
Molly Dunn
Danvers, Massachusetts

Agnes Lesnick
Hillside, Illinois

Rita Soto
Chicago, Illinois

Grade 3
Jane Curran
Honesdale, Pennsylvania

Sandra Tucker
Chicago, Illinois

Grade 4
Sara Stoneberg Llibre
Chicago, Illinois

Sheri Roedel
Chicago, Illinois

Grade 5
Todd Atler
Chicago, Illinois

Leah Barry
Norfolk, Massachusetts

Special Thanks
Special thanks to the many teachers, students, parents, principals, writers, researchers, and work-study students who participated in the Children's Math Worlds Research Project over the years.

Credits
Cover art: (stopwatch) © Photodisc/Getty Images. (cheetah) © John Daniels/Ardea London Ltd. (train) © Michael Dunning/Photographer's Choice/Getty Images.

Illustrative art: Dave Klug
Technical art: Morgan-Cain & Associates

Copyright © 2008 by Houghton Mifflin Company. All rights reserved.

No part of this work may be reproduced or transmitted in any form or by any means, electronic or mechanical, including photocopying or recording, or by any information storage or retrieval system without the prior written permission of the copyright owner unless such copying is expressly permitted by federal copyright law. With the exception of nonprofit transcription into Braille, Houghton Mifflin is not authorized to grant permission for further uses of this work. Permission must be obtained from the individual copyright owner as identified herein. Address requests for permission to make copies of Houghton Mifflin material to School Permissions, Houghton Mifflin Company, 222 Berkeley Street, Boston, MA 02116.

Printed in the U.S.A.

ISBN-13: 978-0-618-89616-5
ISBN-10: 0-618-89616-3

2 3 4 5 6 7 8 9 KDL 11 10 09 08

VOLUME 2 CONTENTS

Unit 4 Multi-Digit Multiplication and Division

Multiplication With Whole Numbers

1 Shift Patterns in Multiplication 237
    FAMILY LETTER 243

2 The Rectangle Sections Method for Multiplication 245

3 Multiply Two-Digit Numbers 247
   Going Further 250

4 Multiply With Larger Numbers 251

5 Patterns With Fives and Zeros 253

6 Multiplication Practice 255
   Going Further 256

Multiplication With Decimal Numbers

7 Multiply Decimals by Whole Numbers 257
   Going Further 260

8 Multiply by Decimals 261

9 Compare Shift Patterns 267

10 Estimate Products 269

11 Multiplication Practice 273
    Going Further 275

One-Digit Divisors

12 Divide Whole Numbers by One Digit 277
    Going Further 279

13 Divide Decimal Numbers by One Digit 281

14 Express Fractions as Decimals 283
    Going Further 286

Two-Digit Divisors

15 Explore Dividing by Two-Digit Whole Numbers 287

16 Too Large, Too Small, or Just Right? 289

17 Interpret Remainders 291

18 Divide Whole Numbers by Decimal Numbers 295

19 Divide With Two Decimal Numbers . 301
    Going Further 305

20 Division Practice 307

21 Distinguish Between Multiplication and Division 311

✓ **UNIT 4** Test 317

VOLUME 2 CONTENTS (CONTINUED)

Mini Unit D The Coordinate Plane

1 Explore Transformations 319
   FAMILY LETTER 325

2 Coordinate Graphs in the
   First Quadrant 327
   Going Further 330
3 Graph Functions 331
   Going Further 334
4 Negative Numbers 335
5 Pattern Day . . . . *
✓ UNIT D Test 337

Unit 5 Multiplication and Division With Fractions

Multiplication With Fractions

1 Basic Multiplication Concepts 339
   FAMILY LETTER 341

2 Multiplication With Non-Unit
   Fractions 343
3 Multiplication With Fractional
   Solutions 345
4 Multiply a Fraction by a Fraction . . . *
5 Multiplication Strategies 347

Multiplication Links

6 Relate Fractional Operations 349
7 Find Decimal Equivalents
   of Fractions 351
   Going Further 352
8 When Dividing Is Also
   Multiplying 353
9 Mixed Practice With Fractions 355

Dividing With Fractions

10 Explore Fractional Division 357
11 Division as Reverse Multiplication . 359
12 Investigate Division by Inversion . . 361
13 Distinguish Multiplication
   From Division 363
14 Review Operations With Fractions . 367
✓ UNIT 5 Test 369

* This lesson consists only of activities from the Teacher's Guide.

VOLUME 2 CONTENTS (CONTINUED)

Mini Unit E Three-Dimensional and Two-Dimensional Relationships

1 Prisms and Cylinders 371
    FAMILY LETTER 377

2 Pyramids and Cones 379
3 Compare and Contrast Geometric Solids 385
✓ **UNIT E** Test 387

Unit 6 Ratio, Proportion, and Percent

Ratio and Proportion

1 Multiplication Patterns 389
    FAMILY LETTER 393

2 Unit Rate 395
3 What Is a Multiplication Column Situation? 397
4 Linked Stories Are Ratios 399
5 What Are Proportion Situations? . . 403
6 Solve Proportion Problems 407
7 Solve Proportions as Factor Puzzles 409
8 Basic Ratios 411
9 Write and Solve Proportion Problems 413

Percent

10 The Meaning of Percent 415
11 Solve Problems Using Percents . . . 419
12 Probability Using Percents and Decimals 423
✓ **UNIT 6** Test 425

VOLUME 2 CONTENTS (CONTINUED)

Mini Unit F Proportion and Measurement

1 Similar Figures **427**
    Going Further. **430**
    FAMILY LETTER **433**

2 Map Scales **435**
3 Explore Scale Drawings **437**
4 Use Scale Drawings **439**
✓ **UNIT F** Test **441**
Glossary **S1**

* This lesson consists only of activities from the Teacher's Guide.

▶ Shifts With Whole Numbers

Jordan earns $243 a week. The money is shown at the right. Answer the questions about how much he will earn over time.

Jordan's Weekly Earnings

$ ____ ____ ____ 2 4 3

× 1

1 × $243 = $243

1. After 10 weeks, how much will Jordan have earned?

   _____

2. What happens to each $1-bill when it is multiplied by 10?

   _____

3. What happens to each other bill when it is multiplied by 10?

   _____

4. When you multiply by 10, does each digit shift to the right or left?

   _____

5. How many places does each digit shift?

   _____

After 10 Weeks

$ ____ ____ 2 , 4 3 0

× 10

10 × $243 = $2,430

UNIT 4 LESSON 1   CA Standards: NS 1.0; MR 1.1, 2.3   Shift Patterns in Multiplication **237**

6. After 100 weeks, how much will Jordan have earned?

   _____

After 100 Weeks

$ ____ 2 4 , 3 0 0

× 100

10 × 10 × $243 = $24,300

7. What happens to each $1-bill when it is multiplied by 100?

   _____

8. What happens to each digit when it is multiplied by 100?

   _____

9. When you multiply by 100, does each digit shift to the right or left?

   _____

10. How many places does each digit shift?

    _____

11. After 1,000 weeks, how much will Jordan have earned?

    _____

After 1,000 Weeks

$ 2 4 3 , 0 0 0

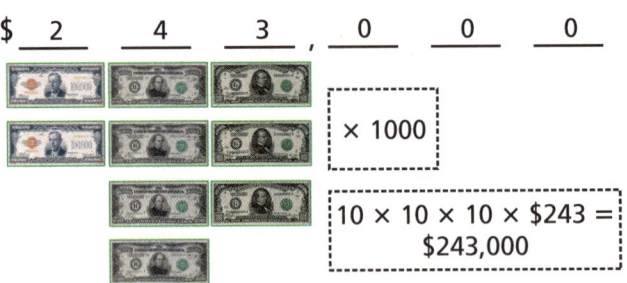

× 1000

10 × 10 × 10 × $243 = $243,000

12. What happens to each $1-bill when it is multiplied by 1,000?

    _____

13. What happens to each digit when it is multiplied by 1,000?

    _____

14. When you multiply by 1,000, does each digit shift to the right or left?

    _____

15. How many places does each digit shift?

    _____

4-1 Class Activity

Name _____ Date _____

▶ See the Shift in Motion

Isabel earns $325 a week. Three students can show how the digits shift at the board when we multiply her earnings.

Complete each exercise.

16. Suppose Isabel works for 10 weeks. Find her earnings.

___ ___ ___ $3 2 5 [× 10] ▷ $___ ___ 3 , 2 5 0

$325 shifts ___ place(s) to the ___. It gets 10 times as great.

17. Suppose Isabel works for 100 weeks. Find her earnings.

___ ___ ___ $3 2 5 [× 100] ▷ $___ 3 2 , 5 0 0

$325 shifts ___ places to the ___. It gets 100 times as great.

18. Suppose Isabel works for 1,000 weeks. Find her earnings.

___ ___ ___ $3 2 5 [× 1,000] ▷ $3 2 5 , 0 0 0

$325 shifts ___ places to the ___. It gets 1,000 times as great.

Complete each exercise.

19. 567 × 10 = _____

20. 38 × 1,000 = _____

21. 912 × 100 = _____

22. 700 × 10 = _____

23. The Skyway Express train travels about 800 miles a day. How far does it travel in 10 days?

_____

24. If there are 30 days in April, about how far will the train travel during the month of April?

_____

UNIT 4 LESSON 1   CA Standards: NS 1.0; MR 1.1, 2.3, 3.2   Shift Patterns in Multiplication **239**

4-1 Class Activity

Name _____ **Date** _____

▶ Shifts With Decimal Amounts

It costs $0.412 (41 and 2/10 cents) for a factory to make a Red Phantom marble. The money is shown here.

Cost of a Red Phantom Marble

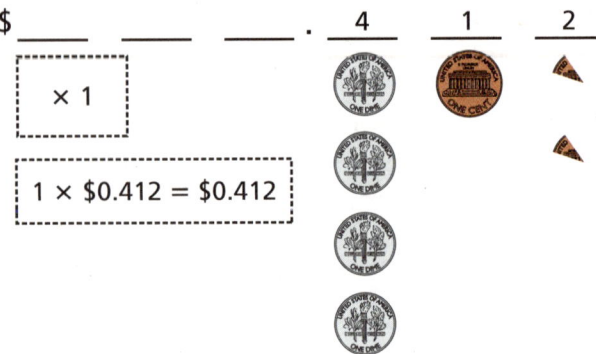

× 1

1 × $0.412 = $0.412

Answer each question about the cost of making different numbers of Red Phantom marbles.

25. How much does it cost to make 10 Red Phantom Marbles?

    _____

10 Red Phantom Marbles

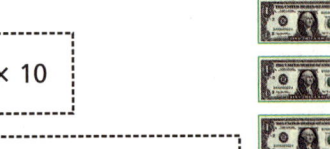 

26. What happens to each coin when it is multiplied by 10?

    _____

    × 10

27. What happens to each digit?

    _____

    10 × $0.412 = $4.12

28. When you multiply by 10, does each digit shift to the right or left?

    _____

29. How many places does each digit shift?

    _____

240 UNIT 4 LESSON 1   CA Standards: NS 2.0; MR 1.1, 2.3   Shift Patterns in Multiplication

Name _____ Date _____

30. How much does it cost to make 100 Red Phantom Marbles?

    _____

31. What happens to each coin when you multiply by 100?

    _____

32. What happens to each digit?

    _____

100 Red Phantom Marbles

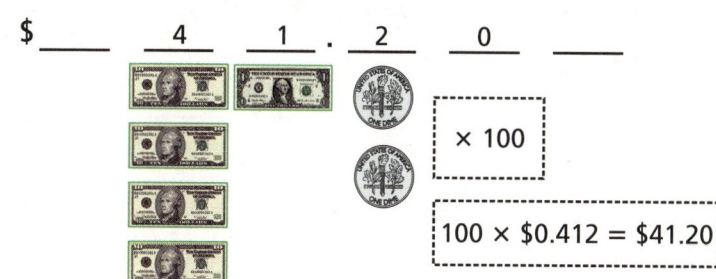

$ ____ 4   1 . 2   0 ____

× 100

100 × $0.412 = $41.20

33. When you multiply by 100, does each digit shift to the right or left?

    _____

34. How many places does each digit shift?

    _____

35. How much does it cost to make 1,000 Red Phantom Marbles?

    _____

36. What happens to each coin when you multiply by 1,000?

    _____

1,000 Red Phantom Marbles

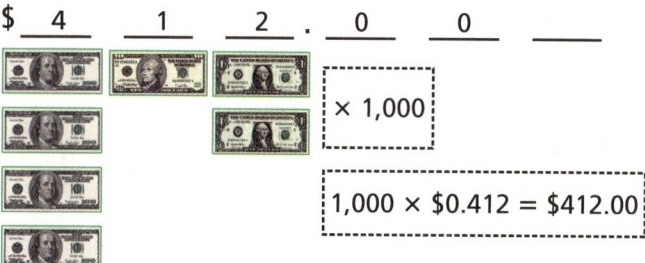

$ ____ 4   1   2 . 0   0 ____

× 1,000

1,000 × $0.412 = $412.00

37. What happens to each digit?

    _____

38. When you multiply by 1,000, does each digit shift to the right or left?

    _____

39. How many places does each digit shift?

    _____

UNIT 4 LESSON 1   CA Standards: NS 2.0; MR 1.1, 2.3   Shift Patterns in Multiplication **241**

4-1 Class Activity

▶ Patterns in Multiplying With Zeros

Discuss patterns you see across each row and down each column. Then state the Big Idea for multiplying numbers with zeros.

×	3	30	300	3,000
2	a. 2 × 3 = 6	b. 2 × 30 = 2 × 3 × 10 = 6 × 10 = 60	c. 2 × 300 = 2 × 3 × 100 = 6 × 100 = 600	d. 2 × 3,000 = 2 × 3 × 1,000 = 6 × 1,000 = 6,000
20	e. 20 × 3 = 2 × 10 × 3 = 6 × 10 = 60	f. 20 × 30 = 2 × 10 × 3 × 10 = 6 × 100 = 600	g. 20 × 300 = 2 × 10 × 3 × 100 = 6 × 1,000 = 6,000	h. 20 × 3,000 = 2 × 10 × 3 × 1,000 = 6 × 10,000 = 60,000
200	i. 200 × 3 = 2 × 100 × 3 = 6 × 100 = 600	j. 200 × 30 = 2 × 100 × 3 × 10 = 6 × 1,000 = 6,000	k. 200 × 300 = 2 × 100 × 3 × 100 = 6 × 10,000 = 60,000	l. 200 × 3,000 = 2 × 100 × 3 × 1,000 = 6 × 100,000 = 600,000
2,000	m. 2,000 × 3 = 2 × 1,000 × 3 = 6 × 1,000 = 6,000	n. 2,000 × 30 = 2 × 1,000 × 3 × 10 = 6 × 10,000 = 60,000	o. 2,000 × 300 = 2 × 1,000 × 3 × 100 = 6 × 100,000 = 600,000	p. 2,000 × 3,000 = 2 × 1,000 × 3 × 1,000 = 6 × 1,000,000 = 6,000,000

40. Big Idea: _____

Solve.

41. 60 × 3

42. 60 × 30

43. 600 × 30

44. 600 × 300

45. 6,000 × 30

Shift Patterns in Multiplication

Dear Family,

Your child worked with multiplication and division problems in Unit 1. Unit 4 of *Math Expressions* guides students as they deepen and extend their mastery of these operations. The main goal of this unit is to enhance skills in multiplying and dividing with whole numbers and decimal numbers. Some additional goals are:

- to solve real-world application problems,
- to use patterns as an aid in calculating,
- to use estimation to check the reasonableness of answers,
- to understand how to convert fractions to decimals, and
- to interpret remainders.

Your child will learn and practice techniques such as Rectangle Sections, Expanded Notation, and Shift Patterns to gain speed and accuracy in multi-digit and decimal multiplication and division. Money examples will be used in multiplication and division with decimals.

Your child will learn to round and estimate, and then adjust the estimated number. Remainders will be interpreted in real-world contexts, and expressed as fractions or decimals. Students will divide by decimal numbers, and learn to distinguish between multiplication and division when there are decimal numbers.

Throughout Unit 4, your child will solve real-world application problems that require multi-digit multiplication and division. Your child may need more work with the multiplication table, so please support practice with the Target and Multiplication Tables and Division Cards.

If you have any questions, please call or write to me.

Sincerely,
Your Child's Teacher

Estimada familia:

Su niño ya ha estudiado problemas de multiplicación y división en años anteriores. La Unidad 4 de *Math Expressions* guía a los estudiantes mientras profundizan y amplían su dominio de estas operaciones. El objetivo principal de la unidad es reforzar las destrezas de multiplicación y división con números enteros y decimales. Algunos objetivos adicionales son:

- resolver problemas con aplicaciones a la vida diaria,
- usar patrones de ayuda para hacer cálculos,
- usar la estimación para comprobar si las respuestas son razonables,
- comprender cómo se convierten las fracciones a decimales, e
- interpretar los residuos.

Su niño aprenderá y practicará técnicas como secciones de rectángulos, notación extendida y patrones de desplazamiento para poder hacer las multiplicaciones y divisiones de números de varios dígitos y decimales con mayor rapidez y exactitud. En las multiplicaciones y divisiones con decimales se usarán ejemplos de dinero.

Su niño aprenderá a redondear y estimar, y luego a ajustar el número estimado. Los residuos se interpretarán dentro de contextos de la vida diaria y se expresarán como fracciones o decimales. Los estudiantes dividirán por números decimales y aprenderán a distinguir entre la multiplicación y la división con números decimales.

En de la Unidad 4 su niño resolverá problemas con aplicaciones a la vida diaria que requieren multiplicación y división de números de varios dígitos. Tal vez su niño necesite más práctica con la tabla de multiplicar. Por favor apoye a su niño con la práctica de las tablas de multiplicar y las tarjetas de divisiones.

Si tiene alguna duda o comentario, por favor comuníquese conmigo.

Atentamente,
El maestro su niño

Name _____ **Date** _____

Vocabulary
Rectangle Sections
partial products

▶ **Solve With Rectangle Sections**

Think about finding the area of this rectangle (Area = length × width). It would be difficult to find 43 × 67 in one step. But if you broke the rectangle into smaller **Rectangle Sections**, then you could do it.

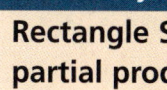

When you multiply larger numbers, you often need to break the problem into smaller parts. The products of these smaller parts are called **partial products**. After you find all the partial products, you can add them together.

1. Explain how Rectangle Sections are used to solve the problem below.

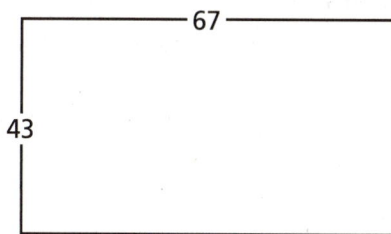

_____

_____

_____

2. Use Rectangle Sections to solve the multiplication problem below.

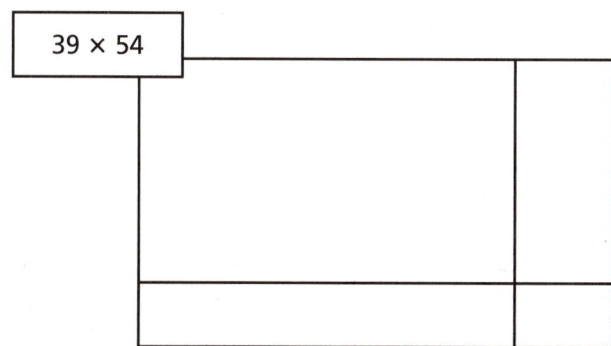

UNIT 4 LESSON 2   CA Standards: NS 1.0; MR 2.3   The Rectangle Sections Method for Multiplication **245**

4-2 Class Activity

Vocabulary
Expanded Notation

▶ Solve With Expanded Notation

Look at the **Expanded Notation** method of solving below. Diagrams A and B both show the Expanded Notation method. Diagram B only shows the results of the steps.

3. How is this method like the Rectangle Sections? How is it different?

   _____

   _____

43×67

A
$$43 = 40 + 3$$
$$\times\, 67 = 60 + 7$$
$$\overline{}$$
$$40 \times 60 = 2{,}400$$
$$3 \times 60 = 180$$
$$7 \times 40 = 280$$
$$7 \times 3 = 21$$
$$\overline{2{,}881}$$

B
$$43$$
$$\times\, 67$$
$$\overline{}$$
$$2{,}400$$
$$180$$
$$280$$
$$21$$
$$\overline{2{,}881}$$

4. This rectangle shows the same problem. Can you relate the rectangle sections (a, b, c, d) to the 4 partial products shown in the Expanded Notation method above? Draw a line connecting each rectangle section to the partial product it shows.

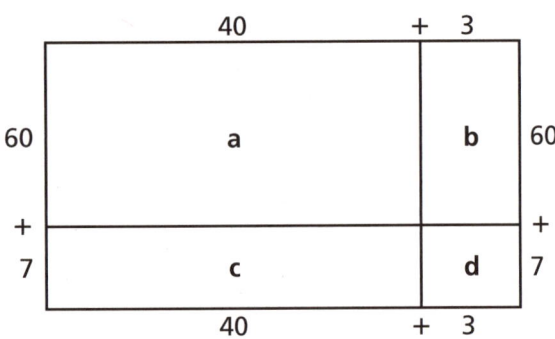

Solve. Use any method you like.

Show your work.

5. There are 32 cattle cars on today's train to Detroit. Each car holds 28 cows. How many cows are on the train?

   _____

6. Maria jogs 21 miles every week. If there are 52 weeks in a year, how many miles does Maria jog in a year?

   _____

▶ Methods for Two-Digit Multiplication

Look at the multiplication problem shown here. It is solved with another rectangle method called **Rectangle Rows**.

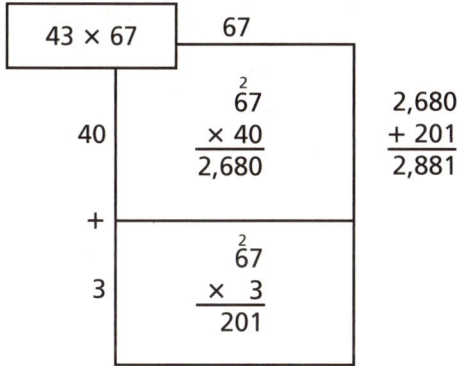

1. Explain the steps of the Rectangle Rows method.

   _____
   _____
   _____
   _____

2. How is the Rectangle Rows method alike and different from the Rectangle Sections method you used yesterday?

   _____
   _____
   _____

Use the Rectangle Rows method to solve each problem.

3. 28 × 34

4.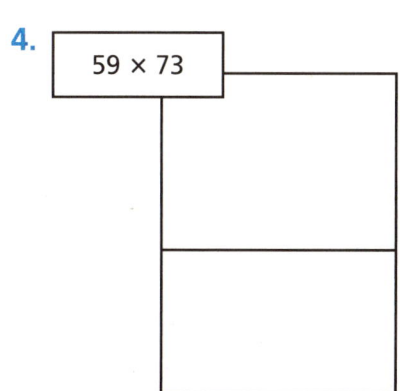

UNIT 4 LESSON 3   CA Standards: NS 1.0; MR 2.3   Multiply Two-Digit Numbers **247**

Vocabulary
Short Cut

Here, 43 × 67 is solved with a method we call the **Short Cut**.

5. Explain the different steps of this method.
   _____
   _____
   _____
   _____
   _____
   _____

6. Why do we begin Step 3 by putting a zero in the ones place?
   _____
   _____
   _____

7. How is the Short Cut method like the Rectangle Rows method? How is it different?
   _____
   _____
   _____
   _____
   _____

248 UNIT 4 LESSON 3   CA Standards: NS 1.0; MR 2.3   Multiply Two-Digit Numbers

Class Activity 4-3

▶ Discuss Multiplication Methods

Below are the four multiplication methods your class has tried. Discuss these questions about the methods.

8. How do the 4 partial products in the two top methods relate to the 2 partial products in the two bottom methods?

9. For the Short Cut method, one way starts with the tens and one way starts with the ones. Could we do the other methods by starting with the ones? Explain why or why not.

Rectangle Sections

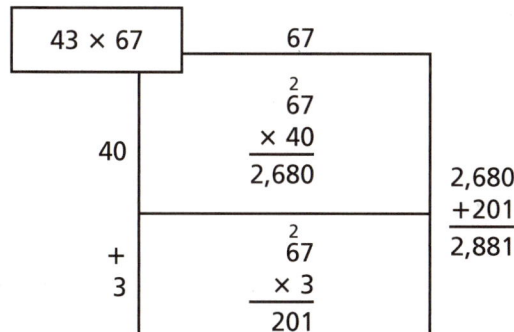

Expanded Notation

```
     67 = 60 + 7
     43 = 40 + 3
40 × 60 = 2,400
 40 × 7 =   280
 3 × 60 =   180
  3 × 7 =    21
            2,881
```

Rectangle Rows

(see diagram)

Short Cut
Multiply by Tens First

```
   2
   2
   67
 × 43
 2,680
   201
 2,881
```

Short Cut
Multiply by Ones First

```
   2
   2
   67
 × 43
   201
 2,680
 2,881
```

Solve.

10. 94
   × 36

11. 73
   × 45

12. 69
   × 82

13. 58
   × 70

▶ Work Backward

Some problems are easiest to solve if you work backward.

Suppose you want to solve this problem: Julian has 5 times as many baseball cards as Carla. Carla has 8 times as many cards as Pete. Pete has 6 cards. How many cards does Julian have?

Answer these questions to solve the problem by working backward.

1. How many cards does Pete have?

   _____

2. Carla has 8 times as many cards as Pete. How many cards does Carla have?

   _____

3. Julian has 5 times as many cards as Carla. How many cards does Julian have?

   _____

4. Look back and check. Write the steps of your check.

   _____
   _____

Work backward to solve each problem.

5. Barbara spent half of her money at the mall. Then she spent half of what was left at the video store. She had $37 when she came home. How much money did Barbara have when she started at the mall?

6. Paul gave Brenda one third of his pretzels. Brenda shared her pretzels equally with Edwin. Edwin had 40 pretzels. How many pretzels did Paul have before he gave Brenda the pretzels?

7. A number is multiplied by 12 and then that result is doubled. The final result is 288. What is the number?

8. You multiply a number by 10 and then divide the result by 5. The final result is 90. Find the starting number.

4-4 Class Activity

▶ Multiply Three-Digit Numbers

1. Below are the four multiplication methods your class has tried. Discuss advantages and disadvantages of each method. Which methods seem better for these problems with larger numbers? Why?

___

___

___

Rectangle Sections

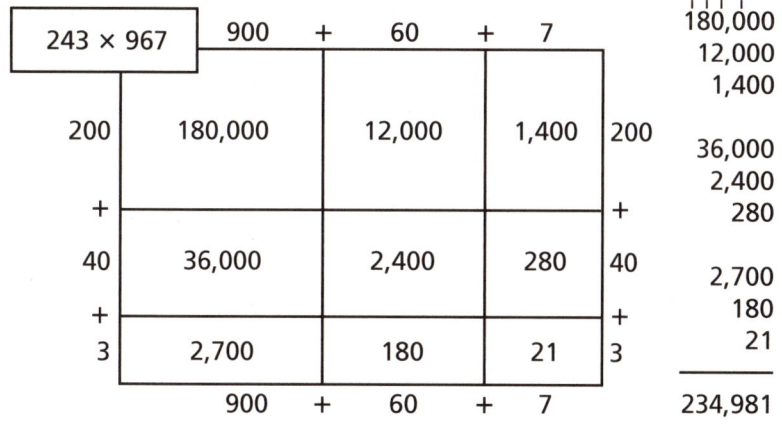

Expanded Notation

$967 = 900 + 60 + 7$
$\times 243 = 200 + 40 + 3$

$$
\begin{aligned}
200 \times 900 &= 180{,}000 \\
200 \times 60 &= 12{,}000 \\
200 \times 7 &= 1{,}400 \\
\\
40 \times 900 &= 36{,}000 \\
40 \times 60 &= 2{,}400 \\
40 \times 7 &= 280 \\
\\
3 \times 900 &= 2{,}700 \\
3 \times 60 &= 180 \\
3 \times 7 &= 21 \\
\hline
& 234{,}981
\end{aligned}
$$

Rectangle Rows

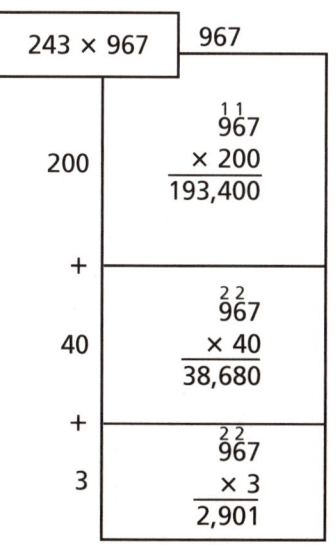

```
    111
 193,400
  38,680
+  2,901
---------
 234,981
```

Short Cut

Multiply by Hundreds First

```
    2 2
    2 2
    1 1
     967
  × 243
 -------
 193,400
  38,680
   2,901
 -------
 234,981
```

or

Multiply by Ones First

```
    1 1
    2 2
    2 2
     967
  × 243
 -------
   2,901
  38,680
 193,400
 -------
 234,981
```

UNIT 4 LESSON 4   CA Standards: NS 1.0; MR 2.3   Multiply With Larger Numbers **251**

Word Problems With Large Numbers

Two scientists went to Egypt to measure some of the ancient monuments there. Help them figure out the information they need to know.

Solve.

2. The Sphinx is a huge statue with the body of a lion and the head of a human. It was built thousands of years ago and still sits in the middle of the desert. The Sphinx is about 80 yards long. If there are 3 feet in a yard, how long is the Sphinx in feet?

   _____

3. The base of the Great Pyramid is a square about 150 feet on each side. How many square feet of ground does it cover?

   _____

4. Some of the blocks used to build the pyramids weigh up to 14 tons. If a ton is equal to 2,000 pounds, how much does one of these large blocks weigh in pounds?

   _____

5. If we include the end zones, a football field is 360 feet by 160 feet. What is the area of a football field in square feet?

   _____

6. The largest Egyptian pyramid covers an area as large as 10 football fields. What area is covered by the largest Egyptian pyramid?

   _____

7. The scientists stayed in Egypt for a year and traveled about 145 miles each day. If there are 365 days in a year, how far did they travel that year?

   _____

Patterns With Fives

1. Write an answer to the Puzzled Penquin.

> Dear Math Students:
>
> I know that when you multiply two numbers together, the product has the same number of zeros as the two factors. For example, 60 × 20 is 1,200. There are two zeros in the factors (60 and 20) and two zeros in the product (1,200).
>
> I am confused about one thing. I know that 50 × 2 is 100, and I am quite sure that 50 × 4 is 200. In these two problems, there is only one zero in the factors, but there are **two** zeros in the product. The pattern I learned does not seem to be true in these cases.
>
> Did I make a mistake somewhere?
>
> Thank you.
>
> Puzzled Penguin

_____

_____

_____

2. Find each product to complete the chart below. One factor in each problem contains a 5. Discuss the patterns you see for the number of zeros in each product. How does the number of zeros in the product relate to the number of zeros in the factors?

_____

_____

5 × 20	=	5 × 2 × 10	=	10 × 10	=	
50 × 40	=	5 × 10 × 4 × 10	=	20 × 100	=	
50 × 600	=	5 × 10 × 6 × 100	=	30 × 1,000	=	
500 × 800	=	5 × 100 × 8 × 100	=	40 × 10,000	=	

UNIT 4 LESSON 5   CA Standards: MR 1.1, 2.3   Patterns With Fives and Zeros

Class Activity

3. Find each product to complete the chart below. Again, one factor in each problem contains a 5. How does the number of zeros in the product relate to the number of zeros in the factors?

_____

_____

5 × 30	=	5 × 3 × 10	=	15 × 10	=
50 × 50	=	5 × 10 × 5 × 10	=	25 × 100	=
50 × 700	=	5 × 10 × 7 × 100	=	35 × 1,000	=
500 × 900	=	5 × 100 × 9 × 100	=	45 × 10,000	=

4. Explain why the product sometimes has an "extra" zero.

_____

_____

▶ Solve Fives-Pattern Problems

Decide how many zeros there will be. Then solve.

5.   80
   × 5

6.   70
   × 5

7.   90
   × 50

8.   60
   × 50

Solve.

9. Ernesto and his sister Dora are playing a computer game. Ernesto has earned 236 points so far. His sister has earned 50 times as many points. How many points has Dora earned?

_____

10. Mount Whitney is the tallest mountain in the lower 48 states of the United States. It is about 14,500 feet tall. Mount Everest is the tallest mountain in the world. It is twice as tall as Mount Whitney. About how tall is Mount Everest?

_____

▶ Computation Practice

Multiply. Use a separate sheet of paper or work on your MathBoard.

1. 35
    × 90

2. 74
    × 40

3. 67
    × 41

4. 18
    × 72

5. 82
    × 76

6. 96
    × 43

7. 153
    × 79

8. 216
    × 74

9. 653
    × 89

10. 584
    × 75

11. 213
    × 479

12. 406
    × 124

▶ Practice With Word Problems

Solve.

Show your work.

13. The planet Mercury has a diameter of 3,100 miles. Neptune's diameter is 10 times Mercury's diameter. What is Neptune's diameter?

14. A movie theater has 16 rows of seats, with 36 seats in each row. What is the total number of seats in the theater?

15. A large package of toothpicks contains 425 toothpicks. If Kerry buys 24 packages, how many toothpicks will she have?

16. Paolo's car can travel 285 miles on each tank of gasoline. How many miles can the car travel on 20 tanks of gasoline?

17. Farmer Ruben's rectangular wheat field is 789 meters by 854 meters. What is the area of this wheat field?

4-6 Going Further

▶ Estimate Products

Vocabulary
estimate
overestimate

You can **estimate** to check if an answer is reasonable or to see when an exact answer is not needed. You estimate to find about how many or about how much.

Carrie wants to estimate 411 × 87. She rounds each factor to its greatest place and then multiplies. 411 × 87 is about 36,000.

411 × 87
↓   ↓
400 × 90 = 36,000

Estimate each product.

1. 68 × 41 _____
2. 62 × 619 _____
3. 57 × 829 _____
4. 309 × 513 _____

Sometimes you need to **overestimate** to be sure you have enough.

Mr. Poy is planning a trip for 64 students. The cost will be $19 per student. To be sure he allows enough money in the budget, he overestimates. He rounds each factor up and then multiplies. By overestimating, he knows that $1,400 is more than he needs.

64 × 19
↓   ↓
70 × 20 = 1,400

Solve. Decide whether to estimate, overestimate, or find the exact answer.

5. There are 21 crates of oranges. Each crate weighs 195 pounds. About how many pounds of oranges are there?

6. Akule's family uses an average of 597 gallons of water per day. About how many gallons will they use in one month?

7. Ms. Long has 12,000 cans of juice. There are 543 students, and there are 18 school days in May. Is there enough for every student to get one can of juice each school day in May? Explain.

8. Erin is making programs for a play. Each program has 9 sheets of paper. Last year, 445 programs were used. Erin wants to overestimate to be sure she has enough paper. How many sheets of paper should she order?

4-7 Class Activity

Name _____ Date _____

▶ Decimals in Money Situations

The Ruiz children had a yard sale. They sold some old toys. They made a table to show how many toys they sold and how much money they earned.

jump ropes	9 cents	3 × 9 cents = 27 cents	3 × $0.09 = $0.27
marbles	2 cents	4 × 2 cents = 8 cents	4 × $0.02 = $0.08
toy cars	12 cents	6 × 12 cents = 72 cents	6 × $0.12 = $0.72
puzzles	30 cents	5 × 30 cents = 150 cents	5 × $0.30 = $1.50

1. How did they know the number of decimal places in each product?

   _____

   _____

2. How much money did they earn?

   _____

Mia saves the change from her lunch money each day. She gets $0.34 in change, and she has been saving it for 26 days. Mia used the steps below to find how much money she has saved so far.

$0.34 = $0.30 + $0.04
× 26 =   20 +   6

Step 1	Multiply by the number in the ones place (6).	6 × $0.04 = 6 × 4 cents = 24 cents = $0.24 6 × $0.30 = 6 × 30 cents = 180 cents = $1.80
Step 2	Multiply by the number in the tens place (2 tens = 20).	20 × $0.04 = 20 × 4 cents = 80 cents = $0.80 20 × $0.30 = 20 × 30 cents = 60 dimes = $6.00
Step 3	Add the partial products.	$8.84

3. How many decimal places are there in the decimal factor (0.34)? How many decimal places are there in the answer?

   _____

UNIT 4 LESSON 7   CA Standards: KEY NS 2.1; MR 2.3   Multiply Decimals by Whole Numbers **257**

A bead factory spends $0.346 to make each crystal bead. The steps below show how Antonio finds the total amount the factory spends to make 222 crystal beads.

$0.346
× 222

Step 1	Multiply by the number in the ones place.	2 × $0.346 = $0.692
Step 2	Multiply by the number in the tens place. (2 tens = 20; 0.692 shifts 1 place left.)	20 × $0.346 = $6.920
Step 3	Multiply by the number in the hundreds place. (2 hundreds = 200; 0.692 shifts 2 places left.)	200 × $0.346 = $69.200
Step 4	Add the partial products.	$76.812

4. How many decimal places are there in the decimal factor (0.346)? How many decimal places are there in the answer?

_____

5. Describe the relationship between the number of decimal places you have seen in a decimal product and the number of decimal places in its decimal factor.

_____

▶ Decimals in Other Situations

6. The owners of the Seven Seas Spice Company want to sell twice as much spice in the future as they do now. The table shows how much spice they sell in a week now and how much they want to sell in the future. Explain how to get the answers by adding.

Cloves	0.3 ton	2 × 0.3 ton = 0.6 ton	because 0.3 + 0.3 = 0.6
Cinnamon	0.004 ton	2 × 0.004 ton = 0.008 ton	because 0.004 + _____ = _____
Ginger	0.007 ton	2 × 0.007 ton = 0.014 ton	because _____ + _____ = _____
Pepper	0.6 ton	2 × 0.6 ton = 1.2 tons	because _____ + _____ = _____

7. Look at the number of decimal places in each decimal factor and the number of decimal places in each product. What pattern do you see?

_____

8. Is this the same pattern you saw in problems 1–4?

_____

4–7 Class Activity

▶ Multiply With Decimals

Look at the patterns you have developed in exercises 1–8.

9. State the Big Idea for multiplying a whole number times a decimal number.

_____
_____
_____
_____

Find each product.

10. 0.8	11. 0.3	12. 0.005	13. 0.14	14. 0.43
× 6	× 40	× 9	× 32	× 64

Solve.

15. Jesse bought 3 aquariums. Each holds 8.75 gallons of water. How many gallons of water will they hold altogether?

_____

16. Jesse wants to buy 24 angelfish. Each angelfish costs $2.35. What will be the total cost of the angelfish?

_____

17. There are three goldfish in one of Jesse's aquariums. Gus is the smallest. He weighs only 0.98 ounce. Ella weighs 3 times as much as Gus. What is Ella's weight?

_____

18. Otto weighs 7 times as much as Gus. What is Otto's weight?

_____

UNIT 4 LESSON 7   CA Standards: KEY NS 2.1; MR 3.2   Multiply Decimals by Whole Numbers **259**

▶ Zero Patterns in Decimal Places

You have seen patterns in multiplying by multiples of 10. You have seen patterns in multiplying by decimals. You can use these two patterns together. The table below shows how you can multiply decimals by whole numbers, using:
- ones, tens, and hundreds
- tenths, hundredths, and thousandths

×	0.3	0.03	0.003
2	2 × 0.3 = 2 × 3 × 0.1 = 6 × 0.1 = 0.6	2 × 0.03 = 2 × 3 × 0.01 = 6 × 0.01 = 0.06	2 × 0.003 = 2 × 3 × 0.001 = 6 × 0.001 = 0.006
20	20 × 0.3 = 2 × 10 × 3 × 0.1 = 60 × 0.1 = 6.0	20 × 0.03 = 2 × 10 × 3 × 0.01 = 60 × 0.01 = 0.60	20 × 0.003 = 2 × 10 × 3 × 0.001 = 60 × 0.001 = 0.060
200	200 × 0.3 = 2 × 100 × 3 × 0.1 = 600 × 0.1 = 60.0	200 × 0.03 = 2 × 100 × 3 × 0.01 = 600 × 0.01 = 6.00	200 × 0.003 = 2 × 100 × 3 × 0.001 = 600 × 0.001 = 0.600

Find each product using the method shown in the table above.

1. 4 × 0.2 = _____

2. 5 × 0.6 = _____

3. 40 × 0.07 = _____

4. 300 × 0.3 = _____

5. 200 × 0.08 = _____

4–8

Name _____ Date _____

▶ Shifts With Decimals

Leon earns $213 a month. The money is shown here. He will save some of it every month.

Leon's Earnings

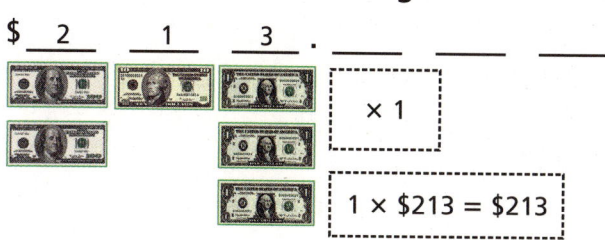

Answer the questions about the different savings plans.

1. If he saves 0.1 of his earnings, how much will he save each month?

   _____

   Save 0.1 Each Month

2. What happens to each bill?

   _____

3. What happens to each digit?

   _____

4. When you multiply by 0.1, does each digit shift to the right or left?

   _____

5. How many places does each digit shift?

   _____

UNIT 4 LESSON 8   CA Standards: KEY NS 2.1; MR 1.1, 2.3   Multiply by Decimals **261**

Name _____ **Date** _____

6. If he saves 0.01 of his earnings, how much will he save each month?

    _____

7. What happens to each bill?

    _____

8. What happens to each digit?

    _____

9. When you multiply by 0.01, does each digit shift to the right or left?

    _____

10. How many places does each digit shift?

    _____

Save 0.01 Each Month

$ ____ ____ 2 . 1 3 ____

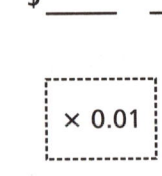

× 0.01

0.01 × $213 = $2.13

11. If he saves 0.001 of his earnings, how much will he save each month?

    _____

12. What happens to each bill?

    _____

13. What happens to each digit?

    _____

14. When you multiply by 0.001, does each digit shift to the right or left?

    _____

15. How many places does each digit shift?

    _____

Save 0.001 Each Month

$ ____ ____ 0 . 2 1 3

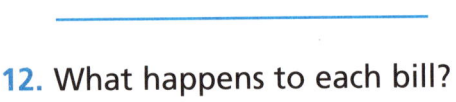

× 0.001

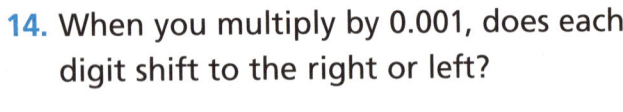

0.001 × $213 = $0.213

262 UNIT 4 LESSON 8   CA Standards: KEY NS 2.1; MR 1.1, 2.3

Multiply by Decimals

Class Activity

▶ See the Shift in Motion

Marla earns $324 a month. She will save some of her money every month. Three students can show how the digits shift at the board.

Complete each exercise.

16. Suppose Marla saves 0.1 of $324 every month.

$ 3 __ 2 __ 4 . __ __ __ × 0.1 ▶ $ __ __ 3 __ 2 . 4 __ 0 __

$324 shifts _____ place(s) to the _____. It becomes _____ as much.

17. Suppose Marla saves 0.01 of $324 every month.

$ 3 __ 2 __ 4 . __ __ __ × 0.01 ▶ $ __ __ __ 3 . 2 __ 4 __

$324 shifts _____ place(s) to the _____. It becomes _____ as much.

18. Suppose Marla saves 0.001 of $324 every month.

$ 3 __ 2 __ 4 . __ __ __ × 0.001 ▶ $ __ __ 0 . 3 __ 2 __ 4

$324 shifts _____ place(s) to the _____. It becomes _____ as much.

Multiply.

19. 24 × 0.1 = _____   **20.** 24 × 0.01 = _____

21. 24 × 0.001 = _____   **22.** 689 × 0.1 = _____

23. 689 × 0.01 = _____   **24.** 689 × 0.001 = _____

4–8 Class Activity

Name _____   Date _____

▶ Shifts When Both Factors Are Decimals

Multiply by one tenth. Think about what it means to take one tenth of another part. You can think about money.

25. 0.1 × 0.4 = _____ Think: What is one tenth of one tenth? Then, what is one tenth of four tenths?

26. 0.1 × 0.04 = _____ Think: What is one tenth of one hundredth? Then, what is one tenth of four hundredths?

27. How many places did the 4 shift each time you multiplied? _____ In which direction? _____

28. Look at your answers. What pattern do you see in the number of decimal places in the products? How is it related to the number of places in the two factors?

_____
_____
_____

Multiply by one hundredth. Think about what it means to take one hundredth of another part.

29. 0.01 × 0.4 = _____ Think: What is one hundredth of one tenth? Then, what is one hundredth of four tenths?

30. 0.01 × 0.04 = _____ Think: What is one hundredth of one hundredth? Then, what is one hundredth of four hundredths?

31. How many places did the 4 shift each time you multiplied? _____ In which direction? _____

32. Look at your answers. What pattern do you see in the number of decimal places in the products? How is it related to the number of places in the two factors?

_____
_____
_____

33. How could you express the Big Idea about the number of decimal places in the product when you multiply a decimal number by another decimal number? Is it the same as the Big Idea for multiplying a decimal number by a whole number?

_____
_____
_____
_____

34. To multiply by 2 tenths or 2 hundredths, you could think of 2 tenths as 2 × 0.1 and 2 hundredths as 2 × 0.01.

$0.2 \times 0.4 = (2 \times \underline{\quad}) \times 0.4 = 2 \times (0.1 \times 0.4) = 2 \times 0.04 = \underline{\quad}$

$0.02 \times 0.4 = (2 \times \underline{\quad}) \times 0.4 = 2 \times (0.01 \times 0.4) = 2 \times 0.004 = \underline{\quad}$

Is your Big Idea about the number of decimal places in the product still true? _____

Use the shift pattern to solve each multiplication. Check to see if the Big Idea works.

35. 0.2 × 0.4 = _____

36. 0.2 × 0.04 = _____

37. 0.2 × 0.004 = _____

38. 0.02 × 0.4 = _____

39. 0.02 × 0.04 = _____

40. 0.02 × 0.004 = _____

41. 0.002 × 0.4 = _____

42. 2 × 0.4 = _____

Using the Big Idea you just discovered, solve each multiplication.

43. 0.3 × 0.4 = _____

44. 0.3 × 0.04 = _____

45. 0.3 × 0.004 = _____

46. 0.03 × 0.4 = _____

47. 0.03 × 0.04 = _____

48. 0.03 × 0.004 = _____

49. 0.003 × 0.4 = _____

50. 3 × 0.4 = _____

Solve.

Show your work.

51. Benjamin bought 6.2 pounds of rice. Each pound cost $0.90. How much did he spend on rice?

52. Sabrina walks 0.85 mile to school. Kirk walks only 0.3 as far as Sabrina. How far does Kirk walk to school?

53. Isabel wrote 4 letters to her pen pals. For each letter she bought a stamp. Each stamp cost $0.60. How much did she spend on stamps?

54. Maura rode her bike 5 laps around the block. Each lap is 0.45 mile. How many miles did she ride?

55. Kim bought 2 pounds of baked turkey that cost $5.98 per pound. What was the total cost?

▶ Compare Whole Number and Decimal Multipliers

Complete each sentence.

Whole Number Multipliers

1. When you multiply by 10, the number gets _____ times as big. The places shift _____ place(s) to the _____.

3. When you multiply by 100, the number gets _____ times as big. The places shift _____ place(s) to the _____.

5. When you multiply by 1,000, the number gets _____ times as big. The places shift _____ place(s) to the _____.

Decimal Number Multipliers

2. When you multiply by 0.1, the number gets _____ as big. The places shift _____ place(s) to the _____.

4. When you multiply by 0.01, the number gets _____ as big. The places shift _____ place(s) to the _____.

6. When you multiply by 0.001, the number gets _____ as big. The places shift _____ place(s) to the _____.

7. How is multiplying by 10 or 100 or 1,000 like multiplying by 0.1 or 0.01 or 0.001? How is it different?

_____
_____
_____
_____
_____

For each exercise, discuss the shift. Then find each product.

8. 3.6 × 10	9. 3.6 × 0.1	10. 3.6 × 100	11. 3.6 × 0.01	
12. 3.6 × 1,000	13. 3.6 × 0.001	14. 3.6 × 1	15. 3.6 × 1.0	

UNIT 4 LESSON 9 · CA Standards: KEY NS 2.1; MR 2.3 · Compare Shift Patterns **267**

Name _____ **Date** _____

▶ Extend and Apply the Big Idea

Zeros at the end of a decimal number do not change the value of the number. Remember this as you explore the Big Idea about the number of decimal places in a product.

These exercises all have an "extra" zero in the product because of the 5-pattern. Complete each multiplication.

16. 0.5 × 2 = _____   **17.** 0.08 × 0.5 = _____

18. 0.06 × 0.05 = _____   **19.** 0.4 × 0.5 = _____

20. Does the Big Idea about the product having the same number of decimal places as the two factors still work? _____

These problems are all the same, but are expressed in different ways. Multiply.

21. 3 × 3 = _____   **22.** 3.0 × 3 = _____

23. 3.0 × 3.0 = _____   **24.** 3.00 × 3.00 = _____

25. Does the Big Idea about the product having the same number of decimal places as the two factors still work? Do your answers all mean the same thing? _____

Solve.   *Show your work.*

26. Ada and her family are canoeing in the wilderness. They carry the canoe along trails between lakes. Their map gives each trail distance in rods. They know that a rod is equal to 5.5 yards. Find each trail distance in yards.

   Black Bear Trail; 8 rods _____

   Wild Flower Trail; 9.3 rods _____

   Dark Cloud Trail; 24.1 rods _____

27. One of the world's largest diamonds is the Star of Africa, which is 530.2 carats. A carat is about 0.2 gram. What is the weight of the Star of Africa in grams?

_____

▶ Review of Rounding

Round each number.

1. Round 42 to the nearest ten. Which ten is closer to 42? _____

   50 ⎤
   42 ⎥
   40 ⎦

2. Round 762 to the nearest hundred. Which hundred is closer to 762? _____

   800 ⎤
   762 ⎥
   700 ⎦

3. Round 0.86 to the nearest tenth. Which tenth is closer to 0.86? _____

   0.9 ⎤
   0.86 ⎥
   0.8 ⎦

4. Round 0.263 to the nearest hundredth. Which hundredth is closer to 0.263? _____

   0.27 ⎤
   0.263 ⎥
   0.26 ⎦

Round to the nearest ten.

5. 46 _____   6. 71 _____   7. 85 _____   8. 928 _____

Round to the nearest hundred.

9. 231 _____   10. 459 _____   11. 893 _____   12. 350 _____

Round to the nearest tenth.

13. 0.73 _____   14. 0.91 _____   15. 0.15 _____   16. 0.483 _____

Round to the nearest hundredth.

17. 0.532 _____   18. 0.609 _____   19. 0.789 _____   20. 0.165 _____

4-10 Class Activity

Name _____ Date _____

▶ Explore Estimation in Multiplication

For each exercise, round the factors and multiply mentally to find the estimated answer. After finding all the estimated answers, go back and find each exact answer.

Estimated Answer	Exact Answer
21. 24 × 39 ≈ _____	24 × 39 = _____
22. 151 × 32 ≈ _____	151 × 32 = _____
23. 0.74 × 0.21 ≈ _____	0.74 × 0.21 = _____
24. 12.3 × 3.7 ≈ _____	12.3 × 3.7 = _____

25. Is there more than one way to round these numbers? Why are some exact answers closer to the estimated answer than others?

_____
_____
_____

▶ Use Estimation to Check Answers

26. Tanya did these multiplications on her calculator.

24.5 × 4 = 98   0.56 × 30 = 1.68   15.2 × 2.03 = 30.856

0.09 × 143 = 12.87   0.74 × 12.02 = 88.948   9.03 × 6.9 = 623.07

How can she use estimation to see if each answer makes sense? Which answers are clearly wrong?

_____
_____
_____
_____
_____

4-10 Class Activity

▶ Ordinary Estimations and Safe Estimations

Dear Math Students:

Yesterday I went to the store to buy 8 bottles of juice for a party. Each bottle cost $2.48 so I rounded to the nearest dollar, which is $2.00. My estimate for the total cost was 8 × $2.00 = $16.00. I had $18.00 in my pocket, so I thought everything was fine. When I went to the cashier to pay, I found out that I didn't have enough money. I was very embarrassed.

Is there something wrong with my math? Maybe estimation isn't very helpful when you're buying things. What do you think?

Thank you.
Puzzled Penguin

27. Respond to the Puzzled Penguin in your Math Journal.

Show your work.

For each problem below, decide whether you need to make a safe estimate or an ordinary estimate. Estimate the answer, and then find the exact answer. Estimates will vary.

28. Michelle and Stacy walked 9.95 miles every day for 14 days. How far did they walk altogether?

Safe estimate or ordinary estimate? _____

Estimate: _____   Exact answer: _____

29. Mrs. Reno is planning to buy 3 bicycles for her children. Each bicycle costs $144.78, including the tax. How much will Mrs. Reno need to buy all 3 bicycles?

Safe estimate or ordinary estimate? _____

Estimate: _____   Exact answer: _____

30. Each bag of soil in the Green Thumb Garden Center weighs 6.89 kilograms. There are 21 bags. What is the total weight of the bags?

Safe estimate or ordinary estimate? _____

Estimate: _____   Exact answer: _____

31. On the Back Explain your answer for problem 29. Which estimation did you choose? Why?

UNIT 4 LESSON 10   CA Standards: NS 1.0; MR 2.3, 3.3   Estimate Products 271

Name _____ Date _____

▶ Practice With Decimals

Suppose you know that 234 × 48 = 11,232. Use this to find each product.

1. 23.4 × 4.8 = _____
2. 0.234 × 4.8 = _____
3. 0.234 × 0.48 = _____
4. 0.48 × 2.34 = _____
5. 48 × 23.4 = _____
6. 4.8 × 2.34 = _____
7. 23.4 × 0.048 = _____
8. 2.34 × 0.048 = _____
9. 234 × 4.8 = _____
10. 48 × 0.234 = _____

Find each product. You may need a separate sheet of paper.

11. 46 × 0.9
12. 75 × 0.8
13. 97 × 0.04
14. 64 × 0.05

15. 0.346 × 127
16. 597 × 0.284
17. 4.59 × 57.3
18. 0.924 × 0.865

Round to the nearest tenth.

19. 0.68 _____
20. 0.93 _____
21. 0.841 _____
22. 0.092 _____

Round to the nearest hundredth.

23. 0.492 _____
24. 0.218 _____
25. 0.907 _____
26. 0.569 _____

Solve Word Problems

Solve.

Show your work.

27. Marcus sails his boat 94.5 miles every day. If he sails for 25 days, how far will he travel in all?

28. The distance around a circle (the circumference) is about 3.14 times the diameter. If a circular table has a diameter of 36 inches, what is the circumference?

29. Nina is reading about red kangaroos. She found out that a male red kangaroo usually weighs about 66 kilograms, and a female red kangaroo usually weighs about 26.5 kilograms. One kilogram is about 2.2 pounds. What is the weight of a male red kangaroo in pounds?

30. What is the weight of a female red kangaroo in pounds?

31. A printer has 395 ink colors and 254 styles of letters (fonts). How many different combinations are possible?

32. Jodie wants to buy a ticket for every basketball game this season. Tickets cost $16.50 each, and there are 15 games this season. How much will Jodie spend on tickets?

4–11

Name _____ Date _____

▶ Use Calculation, Estimation, or Mental Math

There are different ways that you can solve problems depending upon the type of answer that you need.

- If the problem asks for an exact answer then you need to do the calculation.

  USE CALCULATION
  The cost of a movie ticket is $6.25. If 7 friends go to the movies, how much money will they need?
  7 × $6.25 = $43.75

- If a question uses words such as *about*, *approximately*, *almost*, *nearly*, or *enough*, then you can estimate your answer.

  USE ESTIMATION
  Hector earns $8.05 per hour. Last week he worked 19.5 hours. About how much did he earn?
  19.5 × $8.05 ≈ 20 × $8 = $160
  Hector earned about $160.

- For some problems, you can use mental math.

  USE MENTAL MATH
  Angela is training for a race. Last week she ran 400 meters 15 times. How many meters did she run altogether?
  15 × 400 = 15 × 4 × 100 =
  60 × 100 = 6,000 meters

For each question, write whether to use calculation, estimation, or mental math. Then solve.

1. The Math Club is selling packs of paper for $1.95. The first week they sold 125 packs. The next week they sold 376 packs and the third week they sold 408 packs. About how much money did they collect in all?

2. The Math Club ordered 2,000 packs of paper. Each pack contains 150 sheets of paper. How many sheets is this in all?

3. **On the Back** Write and solve three multiplication word problems. Solve at least one by estimating.

UNIT 4 LESSON 11   CA Standards: KEY NS 2.1; MR 2.5   Multiplication Practice **275**

Name

Date

4-12 Class Activity

▶ Compare Division Methods

An airplane travels the same distance every day. It travels 3,822 miles in a week. Compare these methods of dividing that can be used to find how many miles the airplane travels each day.

Rectangle Sections

```
        500                             500 + 40                    500 + 40 + 6 = 546
   ┌─────────┐    Build a new      ┌─────────┬─────┐          ┌─────────┬─────┬────┐
 7 │  3,822  │    section with   7 │  3,822  │ 322 │        7 │  3,822  │ 322 │ 42 │
   │ −3,500  │    each leftover    │ −3,500  │−280 │          │ −3,500  │−280 │−42 │
   └─────────┘    amount.          └─────────┴─────┘          └─────────┴─────┴────┘
        322                             322     42                  322     42
```

Expanded Notation

```
                                          40                    6
         500                              500                   40  ) 546
     7 ) 3,822                        7 ) 3,822                 500
       −3,500        Show the           −3,500              7 ) 3,822
        322          zeroes in the        322                 −3,500
                     place values.       −280                   322
                                          42                   −280
                                                                42
                                                               −42
```

Digit-By-Digit

```
                                         54                    546
         5                           7 ) 3,822             7 ) 3,822
     7 ) 3,822                         −3,5                   −3,5
       −3,5          Put in only         32                    32
        32           one digit at       −28                   −28
                     a time.             42                    42
                                                              −42
```

UNIT 4 LESSON 12   Divide Whole Numbers by One Digit **277**

4-12 Class Activity

Vocabulary: **remainder**

▶ Division Problems

Solve.

1. A farmer has 2,106 cows and 9 barns. If the farmer divides the cows into equal groups, how many cows will he put in each barn?

2. A sidewalk covers 3,372 square feet. If the sidewalk is 4 feet wide, what is its length?

3. Olivia has $8. Her mother has $4,784. How many times as much money does Olivia's mother have as Olivia?

4. A potter can make 2,513 different kinds of pots and bowls by combining different shapes and colors. If he knows how to make 7 different shapes, how many colors does the potter have?

▶ Work With Remainders

This problem might seem unfinished. The leftover number at the bottom is called the **remainder**. We can write the answer like this: 567 R 2

```
       567
   8)4,538
    − 4 0
       53
      − 48
        58
       − 56
         2
```

5. Could there be a remainder of 9 for the problem? Why or why not?

_____

_____

6. What is the largest possible remainder when dividing by 8?

_____

Complete each division and give the remainder.

7. 6)5,380

8. 7)6,747

9. 5)4,914

Find the Mean

Vocabulary
mean (average)
measure of central tendency

The **mean** is one way to describe a set of data. The mean, sometimes called the **average**, is a **measure of central tendency**.

The mean is the size of each of *n* equal groups made from *n* data values.

Stephan found the mean of this data set: 40, 162, 100, 38.
- Step 1: 40 + 162 + 100 + 38 = 340
- Step 2: 340 ÷ 4 = 85
  The mean is 85.

1. Discuss what steps Stephan took and why they give the mean.

Find the mean for each set of data.

2. 24, 27, 25, 24 _____

3. 13, 17, 14, 18, 15, 14, 14 _____

4. 1, 1, 4, 2, 1, 3, 1, 4, 2, 1 _____

5. 350, 400, 450, 100, 500 _____

Solve.

Show your work.

6. Jan's cousins are 144 cm, 150 cm, 131 cm, 160 cm, and 150 cm tall. What is the mean height of Jan's cousins?

7. Mia's math test scores were 96, 80, 100, and 100. What was Mia's average math test score?

8. There are 1,010 students at Ridge School. At Valley School, there are 851 students. At Park School, there are 860 students. What is the mean number of students for the three schools?

9. **On the Back** Write and solve two problems that involve finding the mean.

UNIT 4 LESSON 12   CA Standards: SDAP 1.1   Divide Whole Numbers by One Digit

Name _____ Date _____

4–13 Class Activity

▶ Division With Decimal Amounts

Three friends set up a lemonade stand and made $20.25. They will share the money equally. Study the steps below to see how much money each person should get.

When the $20 is split 3 ways, each person gets $6. There is $2 left.	We change the $2 to 20 dimes and add the other 2 dimes. There are 22 dimes.	When we split 22 dimes 3 ways, each person gets 7 dimes. There is 1 dime left.	We change the dime to 10 cents and add the other 5 cents. Now we split 15 cents 3 ways.
$\begin{array}{r}6\\3\overline{)20.25}\\-\underline{18}\\2\end{array}$	$\begin{array}{r}6.\\3\overline{)20.25}\\-\underline{18}\\2.2\end{array}$	$\begin{array}{r}6.7\\3\overline{)20.25}\\-\underline{18}\\2.2\\-\underline{2.1}\\.1\end{array}$	$\begin{array}{r}6.75\\3\overline{)20.25}\\-\underline{18}\\2.2\\-\underline{2.1}\\.15\\-\underline{.15}\end{array}$

Solve each decimal division exercise on a separate sheet of paper.

1. $8\overline{)47.68}$ 2. $9\overline{)58.68}$ 3. $6\overline{)316.2}$

Solve. *Show your work.*

4. Imelda has 8.169 meters of rope. She wants to cut it into 3 equal pieces to make jump ropes for her 3 friends. How long will each jump rope be?

   _____

5. Tonio has 7.47 pounds of rabbit food. He will divide it equally among his 9 rabbits. How much food will each rabbit get?

   _____

6. Discuss how dividing a decimal number is like dividing a whole number.

   _____
   _____

4-13 Class Activity

Name _____ Date _____

Use multiplication to help you solve these problems.

7. 32 ÷ 8 = _____

   8 × _____ = 32

   8)‾32‾

8. 3.2 ÷ 8 = _____

   8 × _____ = 3.2

   8)‾3.2‾

9. 0.32 ÷ 8 = _____

   8 × _____ = 0.32

   8)‾0.32‾

10. 0.032 ÷ 8 = _____

    8 × _____ = 0.032

    8)‾0.032‾

Solve using mental math. Check using multiplication.

11. 6.3 ÷ 9 = _____

12. 0.15 ÷ 3 = _____

13. 4.8 ÷ 6 = _____

14. 0.021 ÷ 7 = _____

▶ Add Zeros to the Dividend

Jun must run 6.65 miles every day for practice. She knows that if she runs half of that distance and back again she will have run enough miles. How far should Jun run before she turns around to run back?

```
      3.325
   2)6.650     ← She adds a zero to the
    -6            end of the decimal
    ───           number.
    0.6
     .6         This allows her to
    ───         finish solving the
     .05        problem.
     .04
    ───
     .010
     .010
```

15. Discuss whether adding zeros to the end of a decimal number changes its value.

16. Discuss whether adding zeros to whole numbers like 27 changes the value.

17. What is the rule about where you can add zeros without changing the value?

   _____

   _____

Solve each exercise. You may need a separate sheet of paper.

18. 6)‾54.75‾

19. 5)‾141.2‾

20. 8)‾310‾

▶ Write Fractions as Decimals

Fractions and decimals are both ways to show parts of a whole.

1. Divide 100 pennies into 4 equal parts.
2. Divide 100 pennies into 8 equal parts.

3. Write one fourth of a dollar as a decimal number: _____

4. Write one eighth of a dollar as a decimal number: _____

Use long division to write each fraction as a decimal.

5. $\frac{1}{4}$ 4)1.00   6. $\frac{2}{4}$ 4)2.00   7. $\frac{3}{4}$ 4)3.00   8. $\frac{1}{8}$ 8)1.000

9. $\frac{2}{8}$ 8)2.000   10. $\frac{3}{8}$ 8)3.000   11. $\frac{4}{8}$ 8)4.000   12. $\frac{5}{8}$ 8)5.000

13. $\frac{6}{8}$ 8)6.000   14. $\frac{7}{8}$ 8)7.000

Use these number lines to discuss questions 15 and 16.

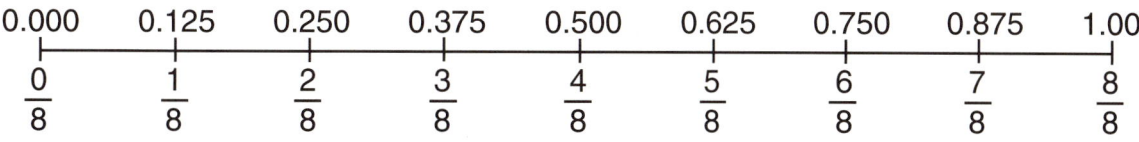

15. What patterns do you see?

_____

16. Which decimal numbers are equal in value?

_____

17. Divide 100 pennies into 5 equal parts.

18. Use long division to find the decimal numbers for fifths.

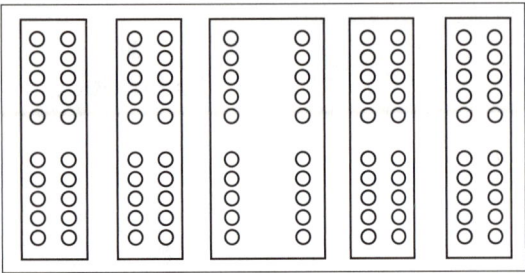

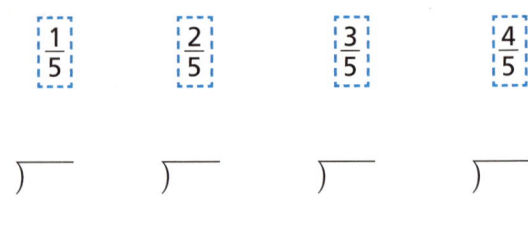

19. Make a number line showing the decimal numbers and fractions for fifths.

20. Divide 100 pennies into 3 equal parts. **21.** Divide 100 pennies into 6 equal parts.

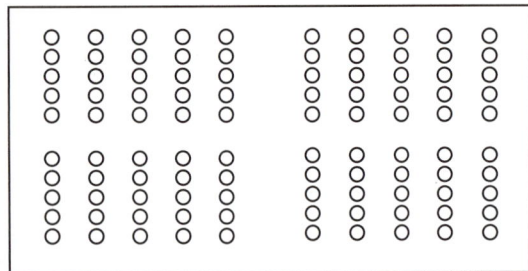
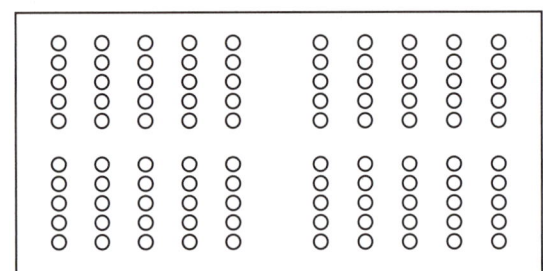

22. Use long division to find the decimal numbers for thirds and sixths.

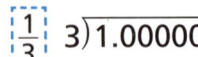 3)1.00000 $\frac{2}{3}$ 3)2.00000 $\frac{1}{6}$ 6)1.00000 $\frac{5}{6}$ 6)5.00000

23. Fill in the number line showing the decimal numbers and fractions for sixths.

284 UNIT 4 LESSON 14   Express Fractions as Decimals

4-14 Class Activity

Name _____ **Date** _____

▶ Word Problems

In baseball and softball, a batting average describes how well a player hits. (It is not a mean even though it is called an average!) A player's batting average is a fraction with the number of hits over the number of at bats. These fractions are usually written as decimals with three places.

$\dfrac{3 \text{ hits}}{9 \text{ at bats}}$

Solve. Give the batting average as a fraction and as a decimal.

Show your work.

24. In the first four games of the season, Lauryn got 3 hits in 9 at bats. What was her batting average?

   _____

25. Felicia is on a softball team. In her first 8 at bats, she got 5 hits. What was her batting average?

   _____

26. On Saturday, Allie played baseball with her family. She had 3 at bats and got 2 hits. What was her batting average?

   _____

Solve.

27. Carl's baseball team had a picnic. The coach bought $3\frac{1}{2}$ pounds of potato salad for the picnic, paying $2.25 per pound. How much did the potato salad cost?

   _____

28. At the team picnic, the players raced on an obstacle course that the coach planned. The first part of the race was on a trail $\frac{3}{8}$ mile long. The second part was on a park road 0.4 mile long. What was the total length of the race?

   _____

▶ Problems Involving Means

The mean (average) of a data set is the equal group that describes the data set.
To find it:

- Add all of the numbers in the data set.
- Divide the total by the number of items in the data set.

```
   3.5
   3.25
   4.125
   4
 + 3.4
 _____
  18.275
```

Tyra is training for a race. She ran these distances last week:

$3\frac{1}{2}$ miles, $3\frac{1}{4}$ miles, $4\frac{1}{8}$ miles, 4 miles, and $3\frac{2}{5}$ miles. To find the mean, she wrote all the fractions in decimal form and then added them and divided by 5. Tyra's mean training distance was 3.655 miles.

```
       3.655
    _____
  5)18.275
```

Solve. Change fractions to decimals if it is easier.

Show your work.

1. Tyra drinks a lot of water on the day of a race. At the last race she drank $1\frac{1}{2}$ cups, $1\frac{7}{8}$ cups, and $3\frac{2}{5}$ cups. What was the mean amount of water that Tyra drank?

2. Sam works at a deli counter. His boss asked him to find the mean weight of the next four customer orders. The orders were: $1\frac{1}{4}$ pounds of ham, $1\frac{1}{2}$ pounds of cheese, 2 pounds of turkey, and $2\frac{3}{4}$ pounds of roast beef. What was the mean weight? Try to solve this with fractions.

3. Tony and his friends sold snacks at the school play to raise money for the Drama Club. They collected $12.50 for muffins, $3.75 for apples, $5.60 for cranberry juice, $12.50 for soft pretzels, $16.00 for frozen yogurt, and $1.40 for carrot sticks. What was the mean amount of money collected?

4-15 Class Activity

▶ **Experiment With Two-Digit Divisors**

Vocabulary
estimate
Digit by Digit
Expanded Notation
Rectangle Sections

When we divide by a two-digit number, we build the unknown factor place by place just as we did before. But now we must **estimate** each number in the answer.

There are 2,048 sheep being sent on a train. Each railroad car holds 32 sheep.

To find how many railroad cars are needed for the sheep, divide 2,048 by 32.

Here are three methods to divide 2,048 by 32. Discuss the steps in each method. Discuss how the methods are alike and different.

DIVISION PROBLEMS WITH STEPS AS SHOWN

Digit by Digit

$32\overline{)2,048}$
(30)
Round the divisor.

$\quad\quad 6$
$32\overline{)2,048}$
(30)
Estimate the first digit:
30 goes into 2,000 about 6 times.

$\quad\quad 6$
$32\overline{)2,048}$
(30) −1 92
$\quad\quad\, 128$
Multiply and Subtract
Bring down 8 ones.

$\quad\quad 6$
$32\overline{)2,048}$
(30) −1 92
$\quad\quad\, 128$
$\quad\quad -128$
Estimate the next digit and multiply.

Expanded Notation

$32\overline{)2,048}$
(30)
Round the divisor.

$\quad\quad 60$
$32\overline{)2,048}$
(30)
Estimate the first digit:
30 goes into 2,000 about 60 times.

$\quad\quad 60$
$32\overline{)2,048}$
(30) −1,920
$\quad\quad\, 128$
Multiply and Subtract
Bring down 8 ones.

$\begin{matrix}4\\6\end{matrix}\Big\}64$
$32\overline{)2,048}$
(30) −1,920
$\quad\quad\, 128$
$\quad\quad -128$
Estimate the next number and multiply.

Rectangle Sections

60
32 | 2,048
(30)
Round the divisor and estimate the first number.

60
32 | 2,048
(30) −1,920
128
Multiply and Subtract.

60 +
32 | 2,048 | 128
(30) 1,920
128
Make a new section.

60 + 4
32 | 2,048 | 128
(30) −1,920 | −128
128   **0**
Estimate the next number and multiply.

UNIT 4 LESSON 15   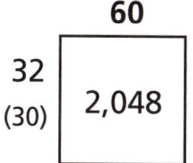   Explore Dividing by Two-Digit Whole Numbers **287**

Name _____ **Date** _____

Look at exercises 1–3. Would you round the divisor up or down to estimate the first number? Complete each exercise, using any method you choose.

1. 79)4,032   2. 21)1,533   3. 18)1,061

▶ Does Estimation Always Work?

Complete exercise 4 as a class. Does the rounding give you a correct estimate of the first digit? Does it give you a correct estimate of the next digit? Discuss what you can do to finish the problem.

4. 54)3,509

Complete and discuss each exercise below. Use any method you choose.

5. 74)3,651   6. 42)3,231   7. 23)1,892

Class Activity

▶ Underestimating

Here are two ways to divide 5,185 ÷ 85. Discuss each method and answer the questions as a class.

```
       5
   (90)
  85)5,185
    4 25
      93  ← What does
             this number
             tell us?
```

```
      10  ← What does
             this number
      50     tell us?
   (90)
  85)5,185
    4,250
      935
```

How do we know that the first estimated number is not right? What number should we try next? Solve the problem using that number.

How do we know that the first estimated number is not right this time? Do we need to erase, or could we just finish solving the problem? Try it.

1. When we estimate with a number that is too big (overestimate), we have to erase and change the number. When we estimate with a number that is too small (underestimate), do we always have to erase? Explain your answer.

_____
_____
_____
_____
_____

Solve each division. You may need to adjust one or both of the estimated numbers.

2. 56)4,032   3. 77)4,791   4. 18)798

Too Large, Too Small, or Just Right?

Name _____ **Date** _____

Think about what kind of divisor is most likely to lead to an estimated number that is wrong. Test your idea by doing the first step of each problem below.

5. $41\overline{)2{,}583}$ 6. $34\overline{)1{,}525}$ 7. $29\overline{)928}$ 8. $16\overline{)1{,}461}$

9. What kind of divisor is most likely to lead to an estimated number that is wrong? How can you adjust for these cases?

_____

_____

_____

▶ Mixed Practice With Adjusted Estimates

Solve. You may need a separate sheet of paper.

10. Hector picked 1,375 oranges in his fruit orchard. He will pack them in crates to take to the market. Each crate holds 24 oranges.

    How many crates will Hector fill? _____

    How many oranges will be left over? _____

11. The skateboards at the Speed Demon Shop sell for $76 each. This week the shop owner sold $5,396 worth of skateboards.

    How many skateboards were sold?

    _____

12. Ashley's dog Tuffy eats 21 ounces of dog food for each meal. Ashley has 1,620 ounces of food in the house.

    How many meals will Tuffy have before Ashley needs to buy more food? _____

    How many ounces of food will be left after the last meal? _____

290 UNIT 4 LESSON 16   CA Standards: KEY NS 2.2; MR 2.0, 2.3   Too Large, Too Small, or Just Right?

▶ Decide What to Do With the Remainder

When you divide to solve a problem, you need to decide what to do with the remainder to answer the question.

Think about each of these ways to use a remainder. Solve each problem. Show your work.

Sometimes you ignore the remainder.

1. The gift-wrapping department of a store has a roll of ribbon 1,780 inches long. It takes 1 yard of ribbon (36 inches) to wrap each gift.

   How many gifts can be wrapped?
   _____

   Why do you ignore the remainder?
   _____
   _____
   _____

Sometimes you round up to the next whole number.

2. There are 247 people traveling to the basketball tournament by bus this year. Each bus holds 52 people.

   How many buses will be needed?
   _____

   Why do you round up?
   _____
   _____
   _____
   _____

Sometimes you use the remainder to form a fraction.

3. The 28 students in Mrs. Colby's class will share 98 slices of pizza equally at the class picnic.

   How many slices will each student get?
   _____

   Look at the division shown here. Explain how to get the fraction after you find the remainder.

   $$28\overline{)98}^{3\frac{1}{2}}$$
   $$\underline{-84}$$
   $$14$$

   _____
   _____
   _____
   _____

Class Activity 4-17

Name _____ Date _____

Sometimes you use a decimal number instead of the remainder.

Suppose 16 friends earned $348 at a car wash, and they want to divide the money equally. To find how much each person will get, one of the friends divided as shown here. Each friend will get $21.75.

```
        21.75
    16) 348.00
       -32
        ‾‾
         28
         16
         ‾‾
        120
        112
        ‾‾‾
         80
         80
```

4. A rectangular garden has an area of 882 square meters. The long side of the garden is 35 meters long. How long is the short side?

   _____

Sometimes the remainder is the answer to the problem.

5. A bagel shop has 138 bagels to be packed into boxes of 12 to be sold. The extra bagels are for the workers.

   How many bagels will the workers get? _____
   Why is the remainder the answer?

   _____
   _____
   _____

▶ Practice Solving Problems Involving Remainders

Solve. *Show your work.*

6. At the Cactus Flower Cafe, all the tips are divided equally among the waiters. Last night the 16 waiters took in $1,108. How much did each waiter get in tips?

   _____

7. A gardener needs to move 2,150 pounds of dirt. He can carry 98 pounds in his wheelbarrow. How many trips will he need to make with the wheelbarrow?

   _____

292 UNIT 4 LESSON 17   CA Standards: KEY NS 2.2; MR 2.3   Interpret Remainders

Solve.

Show your work.

8. Mia must work 133 hours during the month of May. There are 21 working days in May this year. How many hours per day will Mia work if she works the same number of hours each day?

9. Colored markers cost 78 cents each. Pablo has $8.63 in his pocket. How many colored markers can Pablo buy?

10. A meat packer has 180 kilograms of ground meat. He will divide it equally into 50 packages. How much will each package weigh?

11. In volleyball there are 12 players on the court. If 75 people all want to play volleyball at a gym that has more than enough courts, how many of them must sit out at one time?

12. At the Fourth of July celebration, 1,408 ounces of lemonade will be shared equally by 88 people. How many ounces of lemonade will each person get?

13. Armando needs quarters to ride the bus each day. He took $14.87 to the bank and asked to have it changed into quarters. How many quarters did he get?

14. **On the Back** Write and solve two division word problems. Each problem should use a different way to interpret the remainder.

Name

Date

Name _____ Date _____

▶ Use Money to See Shift Patterns

Jordan earns $243 a week. The money is shown here.

Jordan's Earnings in Dollars

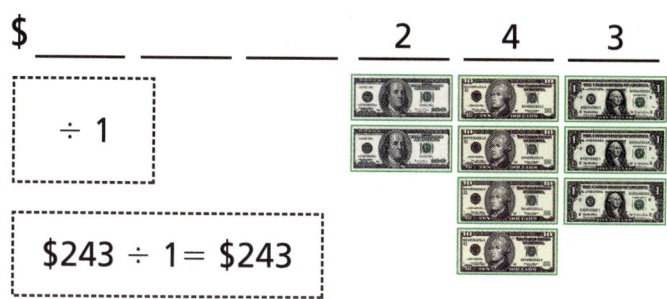

$243 ÷ 1 = $243

Answer each question about how much Jordan earns in coins.

1. How many dimes ($0.10) does he earn?

   _____

   _____

Jordan's Earnings in Dimes

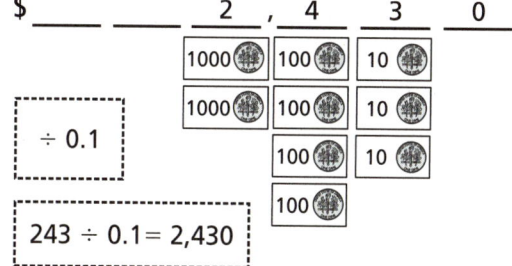

243 ÷ 0.1 = 2,430

2. What happens to each dollar? Why?

   _____

   _____

3. What happens to the number showing Jordan's earnings?

   _____

   _____

4. When you divide by 0.1, does each digit shift right or left?

   _____

   _____

5. How many places does each digit shift?

   _____

   _____

UNIT 4 LESSON 18   CA Standards: KEY NS 2.2; MR 1.1, 2.3   Divide Whole Numbers by Decimal Numbers **295**

6. How many pennies ($0.01) does he earn?

   _____

Jordan's Earnings in Pennies

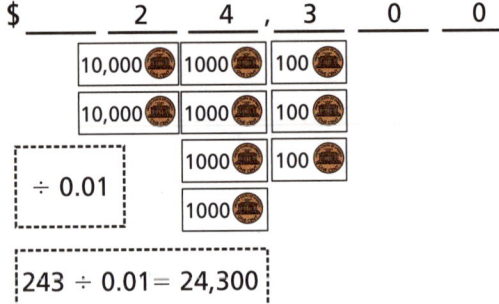

7. What happens to each dollar?

   _____

8. What happens to the number showing Jordan's earnings?

   _____

9. When you divide by 0.01, does each digit shift right or left? Why?

   _____

10. How many places does each digit shift? Why?

    _____

11. How many tenths of a cent ($0.001) does he earn?

    _____

Jordan's Earnings in Tenths of a Cent

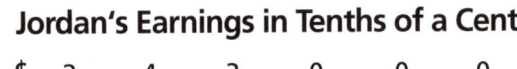
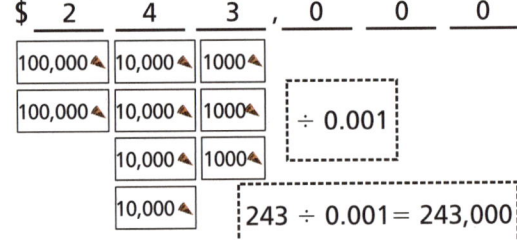

12. What happens to each dollar?

    _____

13. What happens to the number showing Jordan's earnings? Why?

    _____

14. When you divide by 0.001, does each digit shift right or left? Why?

    _____

15. How many places does each digit shift? Why?

    _____

296   UNIT 4 LESSON 18   CA Standards: KEY NS 2.2; MR 1.1, 2.3   Divide Whole Numbers by Decimal Numbers

▶ Relate Decimal Division to Multiplication

Solve.

Show your work.

16. Mrs. Moreno made 1 liter of grape jelly. She will pour it into jars that each hold 0.1 of a liter. How many jars will she need?

Think: How many tenths are there in 1 whole? _____

Complete the equation: 1 ÷ 0.1 = _____

This answer is the same as 1 × _____

17. Mr. Moreno made 2 liters of spaghetti sauce. He will also pour it into jars that each hold 0.1 of a liter. How many jars will he need?

Think: How many tenths are there in 1 whole? _____

In 2 wholes? _____

Complete the equation: 2 ÷ 0.1 = _____

This answer is the same as 2 × _____

18. The Morenos made a kiloliter of fruit punch for a large party. They will pour it into punch bowls that each hold 0.01 kiloliter. How many bowls will they need?

Think: How many hundredths are there in 1 whole? _____

Complete the equation: 1 ÷ 0.01 = _____

This answer is the same as 1 × _____

19. Why do we get a larger number when we divide by a decimal number that is less than one?

_____

_____

_____

_____

4–18 Class Activity

Name _____ Date _____

Dear Math Students:

One of my friends says that dividing a number by one tenth (0.1) is the same as multiplying the number by 10. He also says that dividing by one hundredth (0.01) is the same as multiplying by 100. He thinks this is also true for one thousandth, one millionth, and so on.

Is he right? I don't see how this can be true. Usually multiplication gives us a larger number, and division gives us a smaller number. So this would be very strange. Can you explain it?

Thank you,

Puzzled Penguin

20. _____
_____
_____
_____

▶ Change Decimal Divisors to Whole Numbers

It is easier to divide when the divisor is a whole number. We can change the divisor to a whole number by using the strategy below.

Discuss each step used to find $6 \div 0.2$.

Understand the Division Problem

Step 1: We know that $6 \div 0.2$ can be written as a fraction: $\longrightarrow \quad 6 \div 0.2 = \dfrac{6}{0.2}$

Step 2: We can make an equivalent fraction with a whole number divisor by multiplying the numerator and denominator by 10. Now we can divide 60 by 2. $\longrightarrow \quad \dfrac{6 \times 10}{0.2 \times 10} = \dfrac{60}{2} = 2\overline{)60}$

21. Why will the answer to $60 \div 2$ be the same as the answer to $6 \div 0.2$?

_____
_____
_____

Divide Whole Numbers by Decimal Numbers

Solve with long division.

Step 1: We can multiply both numbers by 10 in long division format. First, put a decimal point after the whole number. ⟶ 0.2)6.

Step 2: Then we multiply both numbers by 10, which moves the decimal points one place to the right. We add zeros if necessary: ⟶ 0.2̯)6.0̯

⟶ 0.2ˬ)6.0ˬ with 30. on top

Step 3: We don't have to draw arrows. A little mark called a caret (^) shows where we put the "new" decimal points. Now we divide 60 by 2, just as we did with equivalent fractions.

22. Why does moving both decimal points the same number of places give us the same answer?

_____

_____

Answer each question to describe how to find 6 ÷ 0.02 and 6 ÷ 0.002.

23. Suppose you want to find 6 ÷ 0.02.

By what number can you multiply 0.02 to get a whole number? _____

Describe and show how to move the decimal points to solve 6 ÷ 0.02 by long division.   0.02)6.

_____

24. Suppose you want to find 6 ÷ 0.002.

Describe and show how to move the decimal points to solve 6 ÷ 0.002.   0.002)6.

_____

25. 0.5)45   **26.** 0.07)56   **27.** 0.8)496   **28.** 0.65)910

➡ **29. On the Back** Explain why your method for exercise 24 is right.

Divide Whole Numbers by Decimal Numbers

▶ Use Money to See Shift Patterns

It costs $0.312 (31 cents and $\frac{2}{10}$ cent) to make one Cat's Eye Marble. The money is shown here.

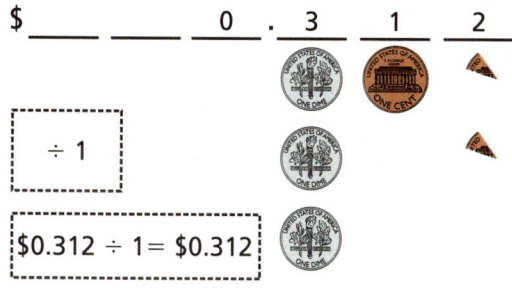

Answer each question about the different coins.

1. How many dimes ($0.10) does it cost to make one Cat's Eye Marble? Why?

   _____
   _____

   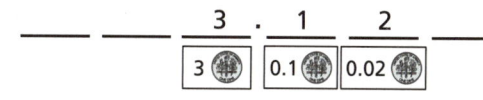

   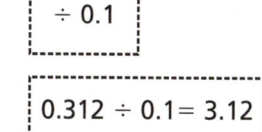

2. What happens to the number that shows the cost?

   _____

3. When you divide by 0.1 does each digit shift to the right or left? Why?

   _____
   _____

4. How many places does each digit shift? Why?

   _____
   _____

UNIT 4 LESSON 19   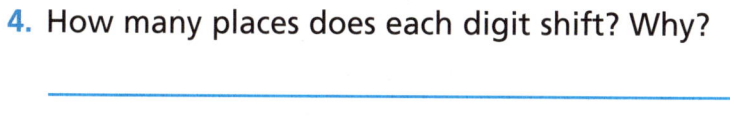   Divide With Two Decimal Numbers

Name _____ Date _____

5. How many cents ($0.01) does it cost to make one Cat's Eye Marble? Why?

   _____

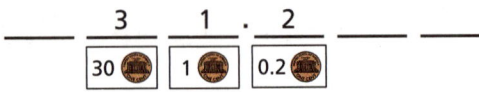

÷ 0.01

6. What happens to the number that shows the cost?

   _____

   0.312 ÷ 0.01 = 31.2

7. When you divide by 0.01, does each digit shift to the right or left? Why?

   _____

8. How many places does each digit shift? Why?

   _____

9. How many tenths of a cent ($0.001) does it cost to make one Cat's Eye Marble?

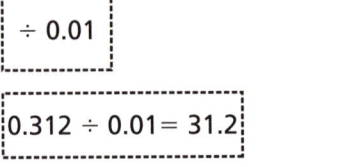

   _____

÷ 0.001

10. What happens to the number that shows the cost?

    _____

    0.312 ÷ 0.001 = 312

11. When you divide by 0.001, does each digit shift to the right or left? Why?

    _____

12. How many places does each digit shift? Why?

    _____

13. Compare the shift pattern in this lesson with the shift pattern in Lesson 18. Is the shift pattern for dividing by decimals the same when the product (dividend) is a decimal number as when the product (dividend) is a whole number? Why or why not?

    _____

    _____

Divide With Two Decimal Numbers

▶ Change Decimal Divisors to Whole Numbers

What happens when there are two decimal numbers? We can use the same strategy as before, changing the divisor to a whole number.

Discuss each step used to find 0.06 ÷ 0.2.

Understand the Division Problem

Step 1: We know we can write 0.06 ÷ 0.2 as a fraction: ⟶ $0.06 ÷ 0.2 = \frac{0.06}{0.2}$

Step 2: We can make an equivalent fraction with a whole number divisor by multiplying the numerator and denominator by 10. Now we divide 0.6 by 2. ⟶ $\frac{0.06 \times 10}{0.2 \times 10} = \frac{0.6}{2} = 2\overline{)0.6}$

14. Why does 0.06 ÷ 0.2 give the same answer as 0.6 ÷ 2?

_____

_____

Solve With Long Division

Step 1: We can show this multiplication by 10 in a long division problem. First, we set up the problem: ⟶ $0.2\overline{).06}$

Step 2: Then we multiply both numbers by 10, which moves the decimal points one place to the right. We add zeros if necessary: ⟶ $0.2\overline{).06}$ (with arrows)

Step 3: We don't have to draw arrows. The caret (^) shows where each "new" decimal point belongs. Now we divide 0.6 by 2, just as we did with equivalent fractions. ⟶ $0.2_{\wedge}\overline{).0_{\wedge}6}$

15. Why does moving both decimal points the same number of places give us the same answer?

_____

_____

UNIT 4 LESSON 19   CA Standards: KEY NS 2.2; MR 3.2   Divide With Two Decimal Numbers **303**

16. How would you solve 0.06 ÷ 0.02 with long division? What number do you need to multiply by to make 0.02 a whole number?

$0.02 \overline{)0.06}$

___

17. How would you solve 0.06 ÷ 0.002 with long division? What number do you need to multiply by to make 0.002 a whole number?

$0.002 \overline{)0.06}$

___

Solve each division problem. Show your work.

18. $0.9 \overline{)7.2}$ **19.** $0.04 \overline{)0.364}$ **20.** $0.6 \overline{)0.372}$ **21.** $0.14 \overline{)7.28}$

22. A sand and gravel company has 12.6 tons of gravel to haul today. Each truck can carry 0.9 ton of gravel. How many trucks will be needed?

___

23. Mountain climbers are climbing a trail that is 3.15 miles long. They can climb about 0.45 mile a day. How many days will it take them to reach the top?

___

Divide With Two Decimal Numbers

Name _____ Date _____

Vocabulary
divisible
even
odd

▶ **Divisibility Rules for 2, 5, and 10**

A number is **divisible** by another number if the remainder is zero when the first number is divided by the second number.

45 is divisible by 5 because the remainder is zero. $5)\overline{45}$ = 9

36 is not divisible by 5 because the remainder is not zero. $5)\overline{36}$ = 7 R1

Here are rules you can use to test for divisibility without dividing.

Rule	Example	Example
A number is divisible by 2 if the ones digit is 0, 2, 4, 6, or 8.	136 is divisible by 2.	283 is not divisible by 2.
A number is divisible by 5 if the ones digit is 0 or 5.	1,760 is divisible by 5.	506 is not divisible by 5.
A number is divisible by 10 if the ones digit is 0.	790 is divisible by 10.	809 is not divisible by 10.

Complete the table. Use a check mark to show divisibility.

		24	65	110	108	137	215
1.	divisible by 2						
2.	divisible by 5						
3.	divisible by 10						

Even numbers are divisible by 2. **Odd** numbers are not divisible by 2.

Answer each question.

4. Write 5 numbers between 50 and 100 that are divisible by 5.

_____

5. If a number is divisible by 10, what other numbers is it divisible by? Why?

_____

6. **On The Back** Challenge: Write numbers that are divisible by 3. Find a pattern and write a rule. Test your rule.

UNIT 4 LESSON 19 · CA Standards: KEY NS 2.2 · Divide With Two Decimal Numbers **305**

Name _____ Date _____

Class Activity

▶ Place-Value Concepts in Division

Dear Math Students:

Today I am going to the store with my friend to buy some greeting cards that cost 75 cents each. I have $19.50 to spend. I want to know how many greeting cards I can buy. I solved the problem as shown below, but my friend said it was wrong. He said that if you moved the decimal points two places to the right, then both numbers will get bigger and so your answer will be too big. Is he right? Why or why not?

0.75)19.50 = 0.75.)19.50. = 75)1,950 = 75)1,950

Thank you.
Puzzled Penguin

1. Write a response to the Puzzled Penguin.

_____

_____

_____

_____

Suppose you know that 1,715 ÷ 35 = 49. Use this to solve each problem.

2. 35)17.15   3. 35)171.5   4. 0.35)0.1715

5. 35)17,150   6. 3.5)1,715   7. 0.35)1,715

8. 3.5)17.15   9. 0.35)1.715

Mixed Division Practice

Solve.

Show your work.

10. The Clark family is having a big lawn party. They have 196 chairs, and they want to put 8 chairs at each table. How many chairs will be left over?

_____

11. Liam needs to buy 640 eggs for a soccer breakfast. If eggs come in cartons of 18, how many cartons should he buy?

_____

12. Jacob made $507 this year delivering newspapers. How much money did he make each month?

_____

13. Ms. Uhura is making 12 skating costumes. She has 21 m of ribbon. How much ribbon can she use on each costume?

_____

14. A class trip will cost $358.40. There are 28 students in the class. How much will the trip cost per student?

_____

4-20 Class Activity

Name _____ Date _____

Solve.

Show your work.

15. The Ramsey family collects and sells maple syrup. Last month they collected 57.8 liters of syrup. They will pour it into bottles that hold 0.85 of a liter. How many bottles will the Ramseys fill?

_____

16. Kyle spent $22.94 on postage stamps today. Each stamp cost 37 cents ($0.37). How many stamps did Kyle buy?

_____

Solve.

17. $0.6 \overline{) 54}$ 18. $0.08 \overline{) 72}$ 19. $0.5 \overline{) 0.45}$ 20. $0.04 \overline{) 28}$

21. $9 \overline{) 65}$ 22. $0.07 \overline{) 0.49}$ 23. $8 \overline{) 76}$ 24. $0.05 \overline{) 34.5}$

25. $7 \overline{) 395}$ 26. $0.6 \overline{) 141}$ 27. $33 \overline{) 3,028}$ 28. $0.045 \overline{) 41.85}$

29. **On the Back** Write and solve a division problem that uses a whole number and a decimal number.

UNIT 4 LESSON 20   CA Standards: KEY NS 2.2; MR 2.0   Division Practice **309**

Name _____ Date _____

Decimal Multiplication or Decimal Division?

For each problem, decide whether you need to multiply or divide. Then solve.

Show your work.

1. A certain turtle can walk 0.2 mile in one hour. How far can the turtle walk in 12 hours? How far can it walk in 0.5 hour?

2. Gus runs 3.6 miles during running practice. He takes a sip of water for every 0.9 mile that he runs. How many sips does Gus take during his running practice?

3. Every year about 135 of the cows on Dixie's Dairy Farm have calves. This year only 0.6 as many cows had calves. How many cows had calves this year?

4. A box of oatmeal holds 1.2 pounds. Each bowl of oatmeal holds 0.08 pound. How many bowls of oatmeal can you get from a box?

5. A rectangular patio has an area of 131.52 square meters. The width of the patio is 9.6 meters. What is its length?

Results of Operations With Whole Numbers and Decimal Numbers

In the equations below, a and b are whole numbers greater than 1, and d is a digit so that $0.d$ is a decimal number less than 1. Answer each question.

6. If $b \times a = c$, is c greater or less than a? Why?

7. If $0.d \times a = c$, is c greater or less than a? Why?

8. If $a \div b = c$, is c greater or less than a? Why?

9. If $a \div 0.d = c$, is c greater or less than a? Why?

Answer each question without trying to find the value.

10. Which is greater, 42×356 or $356 \div 42$? How do you know?

4-21 Class Activity

11. Which is greater, 0.65 × 561 or 561 ÷ 0.65? How do you know?

    _____
    _____
    _____
    _____

12. Which is greater, 832 ÷ 67 or 832 ÷ 0.67? How do you know?

    _____
    _____
    _____
    _____

13. Which is greater, 738 × 66 or 738 × 0.66? How do you know?

    _____
    _____
    _____
    _____

▶ Make Predictions

Solve. *Show your work.*

14. Farmer Ortigoza has 124.6 acres of land. Farmer Ruben has 0.8 times as much land.

    Does Farmer Ruben have more or less than 124.6 acres? _____

    How many acres does Farmer Ruben have? _____

15. Mee Young has 48 meters of crepe paper. She will cut it into strips that are each 0.6 meter long.

    Will Mee Young get more or fewer than 48 strips? _____

    How many strips will Mee Young get? _____

Solve.

Show your work.

16. Roberto can lift 115 pounds. His friend Vance can lift 0.9 of that amount.

    Can Vance lift more or less than 115 pounds? _____

    How many pounds can Vance lift? _____

17. The Daisy Cafe served 18 liters of hot chocolate today. Each serving was in a cup that held 0.2 liter.

    Did the cafe serve more or fewer than 18 cups of hot chocolate? _____

    How many cups did the cafe serve? _____

▶ Mixed Practice

Solve.

18. $0.5 \times 3 =$ _____ 19. $0.007 \times 6 =$ _____ 20. $0.4 \times 0.8 =$ _____

21. $6\overline{)5.1}$ 22. $4\overline{)22.8}$ 23. $27\overline{)8.91}$ 24. $34\overline{)1.564}$

25. 28   26. 0.35   27. 78.6   28. 215
    × 0.63   ×   94   ×   49   × 37

29. $0.8\overline{)7.52}$ 30. $0.03\overline{)0.285}$ 31. $0.42\overline{)15.12}$ 32. $1.9\overline{)1.634}$

314 UNIT 4 LESSON 21   CA Standards: KEY NS 2.1   Distinguish Between Multiplication and Division

4-21 Class Activity

33. 0.37 × 0.09	34. 0.75 × 0.14	35. 51.3 × 6.2	36. 4.29 × 0.27

37. $0.4\overline{)0.156}$ 38. $0.13\overline{)689}$ 39. $0.57\overline{)55.86}$ 40. $0.96\overline{)460.8}$

▶ Mixed Real-World Applications

Solve.

Show your work.

41. The Fox Theater has 19 rows of seats with 26 seats in each row. There are 498 people standing in line to see a movie.

    How many people will get in? _____

    How many people will have to wait until the next movie? _____

42. Polly bought 12 beach balls for her beach party. She spent $23.64. How much did each beach ball cost?

    _____

43. All of the 245 fifth graders at Breezy Point School are going on a trip to the aquarium. Each van can carry 16 students.

    How many vans will be needed for the trip? _____

44. Today Aaliyah ran 4.5 miles per hour for three fourths (0.75) of an hour.

    How far did Aaliyah run today? _____

➡ **45. On the Back** Write and solve two word problems involving decimals. One should require multiplication and one should require division.

UNIT 4 LESSON 21   CA Standards: NS 1.0; KEY NS 2.1; MR 2.0   Distinguish Between Multiplication and Division   **315**

Name _____ Date _____

Name _____ Date _____

Multiply.

1. 30 × 20 = _____   2. 400 × 70 = _____   3. 50 × 60 = _____

4. 0.007 × 10 = _____   5. 3 × 0.6 = _____   6. 0.4 × 80 = _____

7. 47
   × 62

8. 238
   × 65

9. 0.62
   × 93

10. 0.458
    × 71

11. Round to the nearest whole number.   7.52   _____

    Round to the nearest tenth.   0.45   _____

    Round to the nearest hundredth.   0.568   _____

Solve.

12. Paulo's car can travel 38.5 miles on each tank of gasoline. How many miles can it travel on 10 tanks of gasoline?

    _____

13. Jessica earns $85 a week. If there are 52 weeks in a year, how much money will she earn in a year?

    _____

14. Mr. Solomon's cornfield measures 79.6 meters by 34 meters. What is the area of this field in square meters?

    _____

UNIT 4 TEST

Name _____ Date _____

Divide.

15. 7.2 ÷ 8 = _____ 16. 0.63 ÷ 0.9 = _____ 17. 48 ÷ 0.06 = _____

18. 25)̄926 19. 52)̄2,236 20. 1.8)̄104.4 21. 0.29)̄986

Decide whether to multiply or divide. Then solve the problem.

22. Nadia has 38 CDs. She will pack them in cases that each hold 5 CDs. How many cases will she need to pack all of them?

23. The 16 members of the Shady Oaks softball team had a bake sale to raise money for summer camp. They made $740, and they will share it equally. How much money will each person get?

24. Joseph ran 12.5 miles a day for 25 days. How many miles did he run in all?

25. **Extended Response** Explain why when you divide 64.3 by 0.1, the answer is greater than 64.3.

▶ Discuss Rotations

Vocabulary
rotation
reflection

You can rotate, or turn, a figure clockwise or counterclockwise about a point. The **rotation**, or movement of the figure, is measured in degrees (°). Each triangle below shows the result of a 90° counterclockwise rotation about point A, when point A is

    inside the triangle.   on the triangle.   outside the triangle.

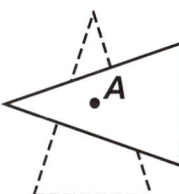 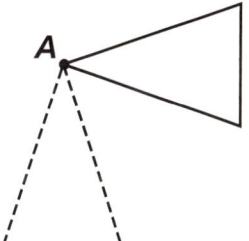 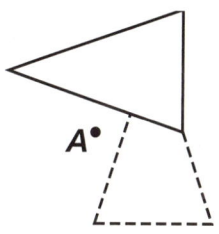

1. Cut out the figures on page 323. Work with a partner to show clockwise and counterclockwise rotations of 90°, 180°, and 270°.

2. Look at two consecutive figures in the pattern below. How many degrees has the figure been rotated? _____

3. Draw the fifteenth figure in the pattern.

▶ Discuss Reflections

You can reflect, or flip, a figure across a line. The line is called the line of **reflection**.

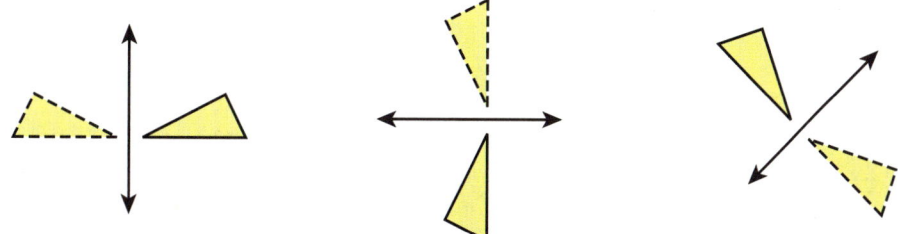

4. Using the figures you cut out and working on a grid, show a reflection across a line for each figure.

D–1 Class Activity

Name ____________________ Date ____________

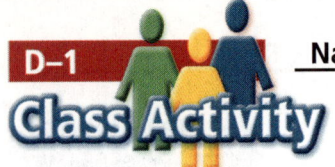

▶ Grid Paper

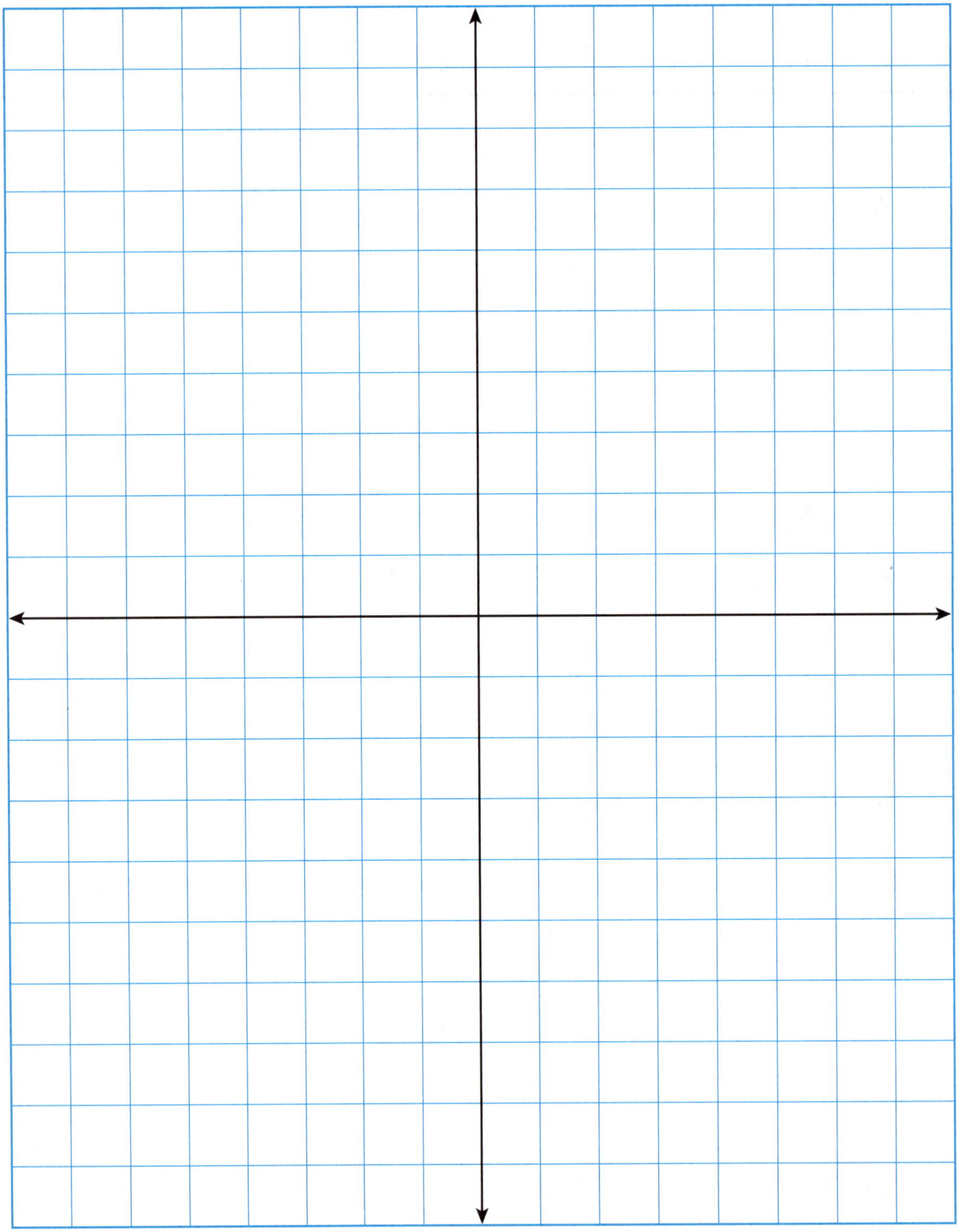

▶ Discuss Translations

A **translation** is a slide. When a figure is translated, each of its points moves the same distance in the same direction. These squares have been translated along the lines.

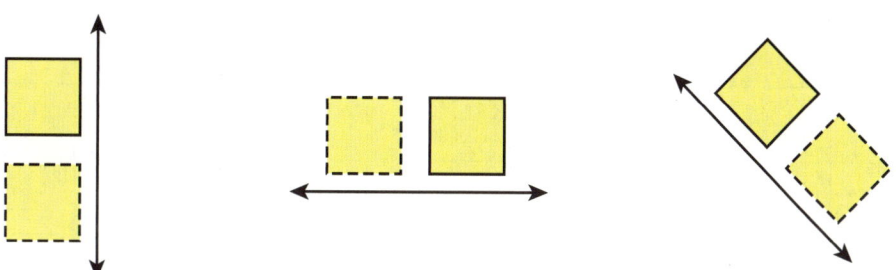

5. Use the figures you cut out on page 323. Use the grid on page 322 to show a translation along a horizontal line for each figure.

▶ Draw Transformations

Draw each transformation.

6. a reflection across the line

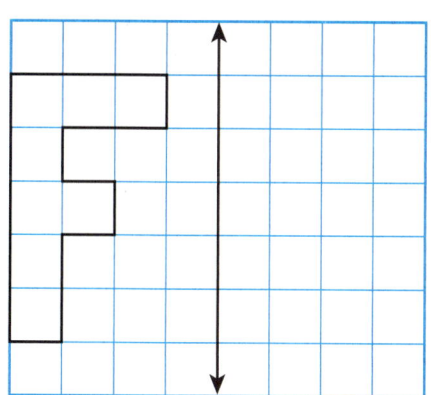

7. a translation along the line

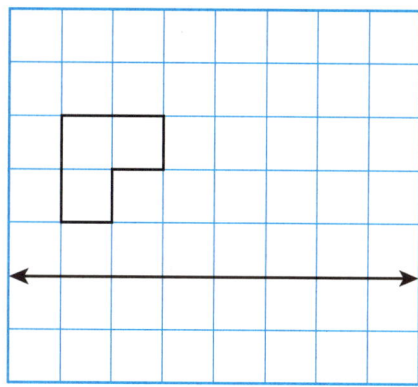

Draw the figure that comes next in the series.

8.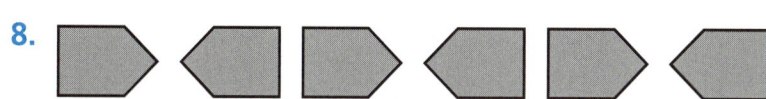

9.

UNIT D LESSON 1

▶ Grid Paper

D-1 Class Activity

Name _____ Date _____

▶ **Cutouts**

Cut out each figure.

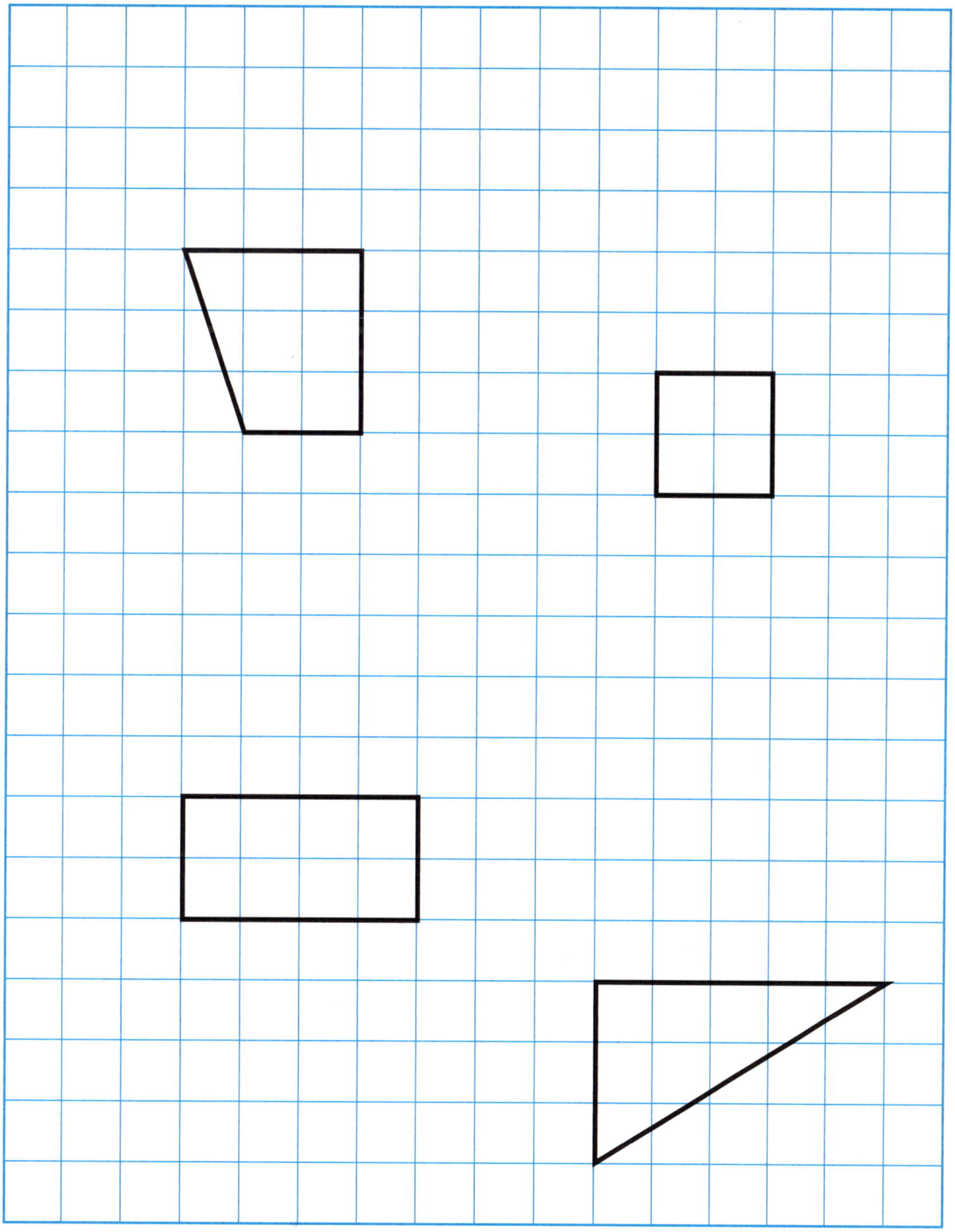

UNIT D LESSON 1 Explore Transformations **323**

Dear Family,

In our math class, we are studying how the position of a shape can be changed. Changing the position of a shape is called a *transformation*. Examples of transformations are shown below.

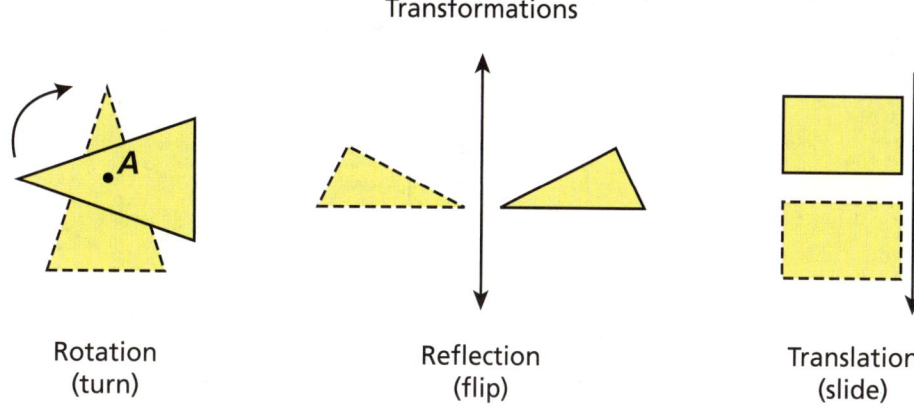

We will also be working with coordinate grids, like the coordinate grid shown at the right.

We will discover that transformations can be made on a coordinate grid. This grid shows a translation of triangle *ABC*: each point of the triangle has been moved two units to the right and one unit up.

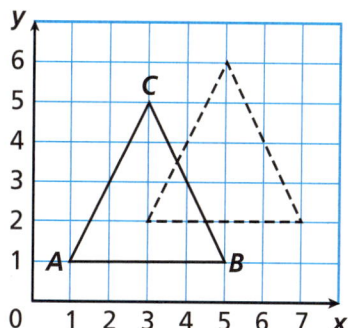

We will also be working with patterns during this unit, and exploring different ways graphs can be used to represent situations in our everyday lives.

If you have any questions or comments, please call or write to me.

**Sincerely,
Your child's teacher**

UNIT D LESSON 1   Explore Transformations **325**

Estimada familia:

En la clase de matemáticas estamos estudiando cómo se puede cambiar la posición de una figura. El cambio de posición de una figura se llama *transformación*. A continuación se muestran algunos ejemplos de transformaciones.

Transformaciones

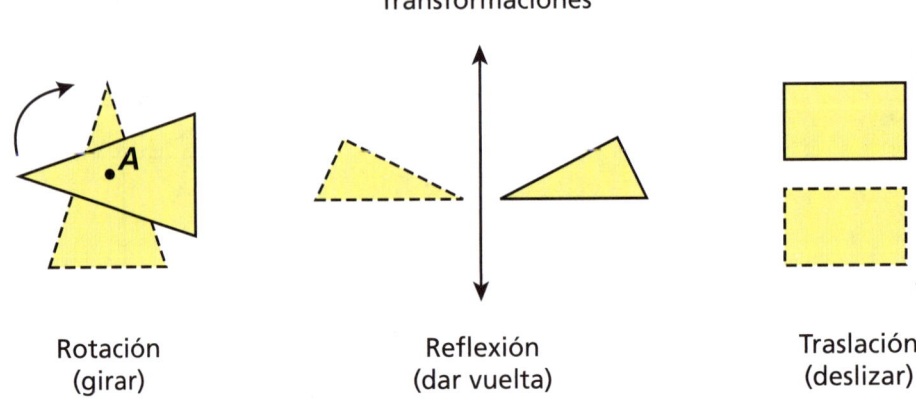

Rotación (girar) 　　　Reflexión (dar vuelta) 　　　Traslación (deslizar)

También estaremos trabajando con cuadrículas de coordenadas, como la que se muestra a la derecha. Descubriremos que se pueden hacer transformaciones en una cuadrícula de coordenadas. Esta cuadrícula muestra una traslación del triángulo *ABC*: cada punto del triángulo se ha movido dos unidades a la derecha y una unidad hacia arriba.

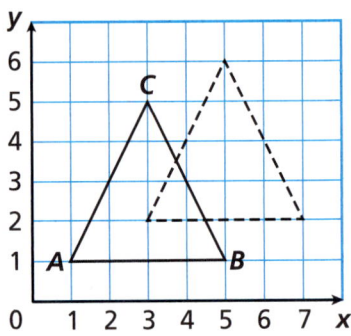

En esta unidad también estaremos trabajando con patrones y explorando diferentes maneras en que se pueden usar las gráficas para representar situaciones de la vida diaria.

Si tiene alguna pregunta o algún comentario, por favor comuníquese conmigo.

Atentamente,
El maestro de su niño

Find and Draw Points on the Grid

A **coordinate plane** is a grid that has a horizontal **axis** (**x-axis**) and a vertical axis (**y-axis**). You can name any point on the grid using an **ordered pair** (x, y) where x and y are the coordinates that represent distance.

Vocabulary
coordinate plane
axis
x-axis
y-axis
ordered pair

The x-coordinate is first. It tells the horizontal distance from 0 along the x-scale. The y-coordinate is second. It tells the vertical distance from the x-axis along the y-scale.

On this grid, the location of point A is (2, 1): 2 units to the right of 0 and 1 unit up from 0.

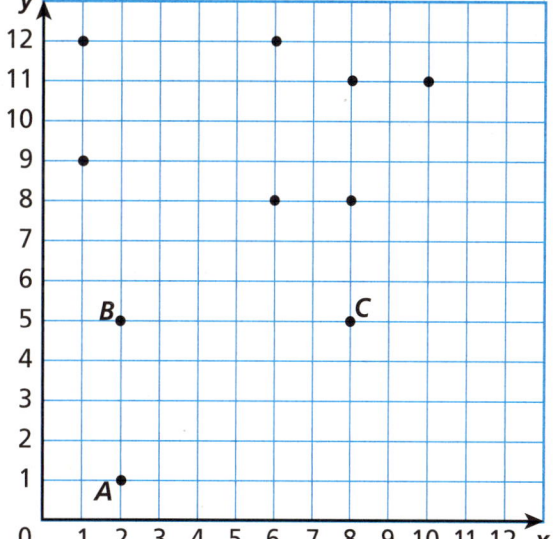

Write the missing coordinate.

1. B is (2, _____).

2. C is (_____, _____).

3. Using your ruler, draw a line segment from point A to point B and from point B to point C. These line segments form two sides of a rectangle.

4. What is the location of the point D that completes the rectangle? (_____, _____)

5. Draw point D and label it. Draw two line segments to complete the rectangle. These are _____ and _____.

Find these points and connect them. Then name the new figures.

6. E is (1, 9). F is (1, 12). G is (6, 12). EFG is a _____.

7. H is (6, 8). I is (8, 11). J is (10, 11). K is (8, 8). HIJK is a _____.

D-2 Class Activity

▶ **Translate Figures on a Coordinate Grid**

To translate a figure means to slide it to a different place. On the graph, triangle PQR has been translated to the right.

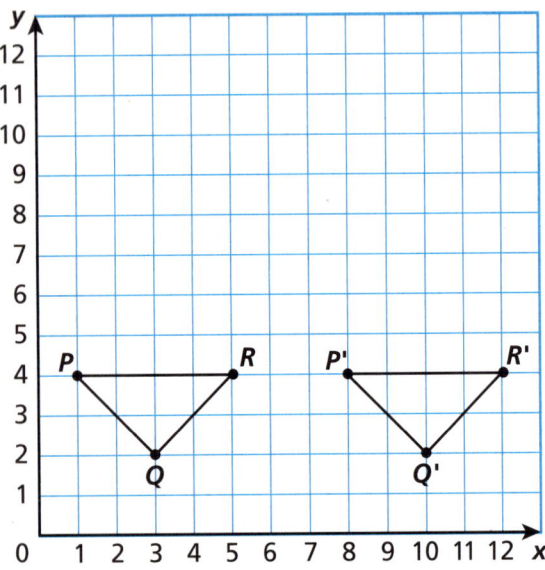

Complete.

8. The distance from P to P' is _____ units.

9. The distance from Q to Q' is _____ units.

10. The distance from R to R' is _____ units.

11. Triangle P'Q'R' has been translated _____ units. The distance between each pair of corresponding points is _____ units.

12. Translate each point of triangle PQR up 5 units on the coordinate grid above. Use a ruler to draw the new triangle.

13. What is the location of each point of the new triangle?

    (_____ , _____) (_____ , _____) (_____ , _____)

14. What is the numerical relationship between the coordinates for PQR and its translated coordinates in exercise 13? Why?

    _____

    _____

▶ Reflect Figures on a Coordinate Grid

When a figure is reflected, each of its corresponding points is exactly the same distance from the line of reflection.

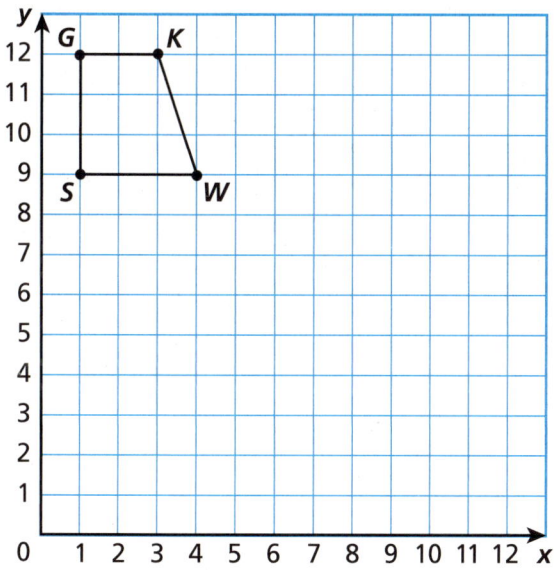

15. Plot a point at (6, 9) and plot a point at (6, 12). Using your ruler, draw a line through the points.

16. Reflect trapezoid *GKWS* across the line you drew for exercise 13. Write the ordered pair for the location of each reflected point.

    (____, ____) (____, ____) (____, ____) (____, ____)

17. Plot points at (1, 6) and (4, 6). Using your ruler, draw a line through the points.

18. Reflect trapezoid *GKWS* across the line you drew for exercise 17. Write the ordered pair for the location of each reflected point.

    (____, ____) (____, ____) (____, ____) (____, ____)

19. Discuss the numerical relationship between the coordinates for trapezoid *GKWS* and the coordinates of the reflections in exercises 16 and 18. Explain your thinking.

Name _____ Date _____

Plot Points on a Grid

Make a square anywhere on Grid 1. With a partner, take turns guessing points to find each other's squares. Continue playing, making the figure listed under each grid.

1.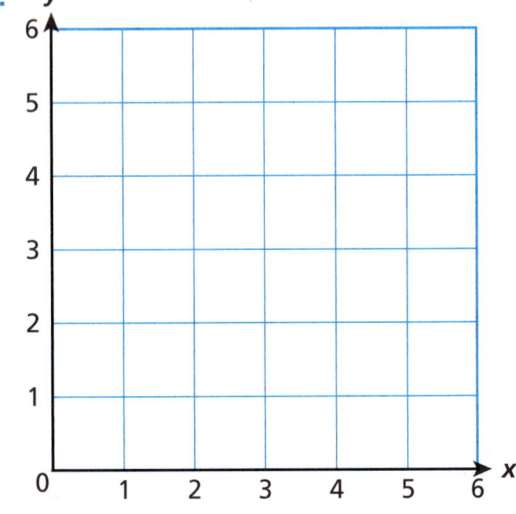

Grid 1: Square

2.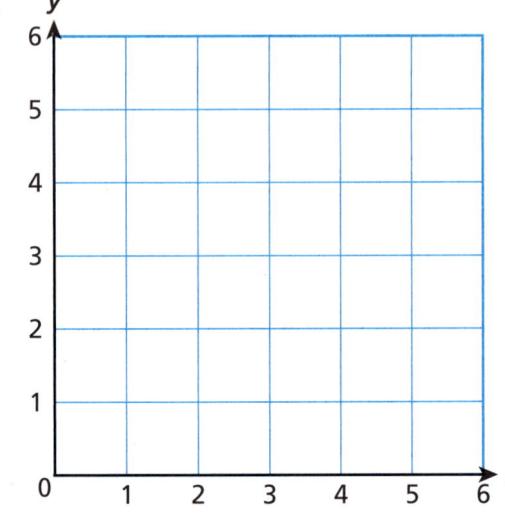

Grid 2: Rectangle

3.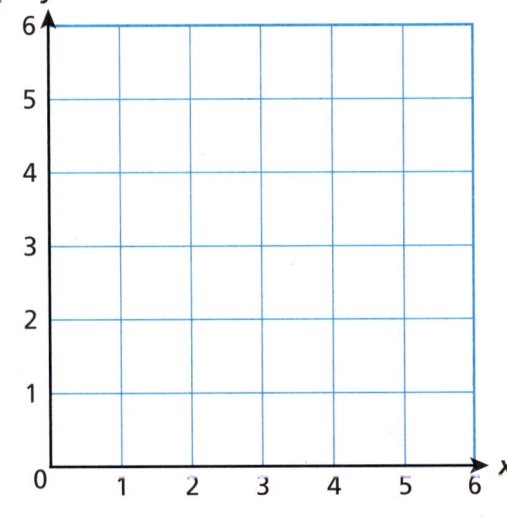

Grid 3: Parallelogram

4.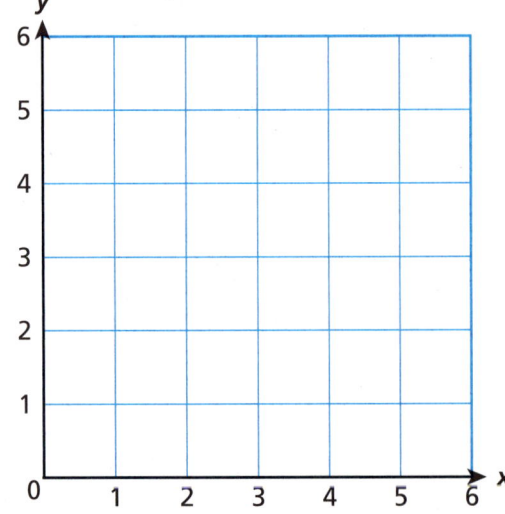

Grid 4: Quadrilateral

330 UNIT D LESSON 2 CA Standards: KEY AF 1.4; KEY SDAP 1.5 Coordinate Graphs in the First Quadrant

Graph a Function

Vocabulary: function

A **function** can be described by an equation, by a table that shows ordered pairs of numbers, by a verbal rule, or by a line on a coordinate graph made by connecting ordered pairs.

1. Mindy and her friends are planning to walk for a charity. They will earn the same number of dollars for each mile they walk. Fill in the 4 tables to show what they could earn for charity.

$d = m$	
m	d
0	0
1	___
2	___
3	___
4	___
5	___

$d = 2m$	
m	d
0	___
1	___
2	___
3	___
4	___
5	___

$d = 3m$	
m	d
0	___
1	___
2	___
3	___
4	___
5	___

$d = 5m$	
m	d
0	___
1	___
2	___
3	___
4	___
5	___

2. For each table, graph the ordered pairs and connect the points with a line (use your ruler to draw the line). Label each line with its equation.

3. Give 2 coordinate pairs you could use to graph $d = 4m$.

    (_____, _____) and (_____, _____)

Draw and label this line.

4. Discuss relationships you see.

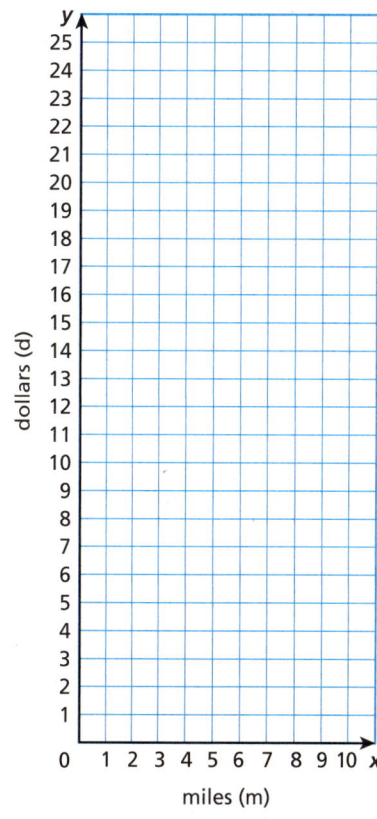

UNIT D LESSON 3 CA Standards: KEY AF 1.4, KEY AF 1.5 Graph Functions **331**

▶ Use a Verbal Rule to Graph a Function

Functions can also describe additive relations. In these tables, *s* is age of a sister and *b* is the age of a brother. Discuss what each table tells you about their ages.

s = b	
b	s
0	___
1	___
2	___
3	___
4	___
5	___

s = b + 1	
b	s
0	___
1	___
2	___
3	___
4	___
5	___

s = b + 2	
b	s
0	___
1	___
2	___
3	___
4	___
5	___

s = b + 3	
b	s
0	___
1	___
2	___
3	___
4	___
5	___

s = b + 4	
b	s
0	___
1	___
2	___
3	___
4	___
5	___

5. For each table, graph the ordered pairs and connect the points with a line (use your ruler to draw the line). Label each line with its equation.

6. Give 2 coordinate pairs you could use to graph $s = b + 10$.

   (____, ____) and (____, ____)

Draw and label this line.

7. Discuss relationships you see.

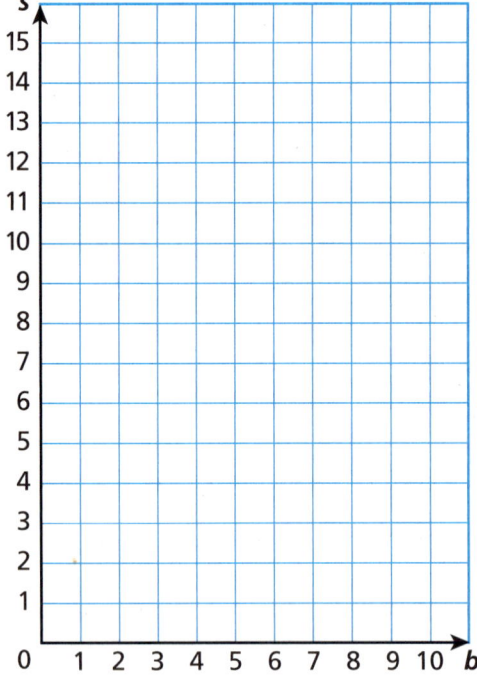

Graph Functions

Patterns in Function Lines

Functions are often given using *x* and *y*.

8. Complete each function table.

9. Write the rule in words for each equation.

   y = *x* _____

   _____

   y = 2*x* _____

   _____

   y = *x* + 2 _____

   _____

y = *x*		*y* = 2*x*		*y* = *x* + 2	
x	*y*	*x*	*y*	*x*	*y*
0	___	0	___	0	___
1	___	1	___	1	___
2	___	2	___	2	___
3	___	3	___	3	___
4	___	4	___	4	___
5	___	5	___	5	___

10. Plot the coordinates from each table. Draw a line to connect each set of points. Label each line with its equation.

11. How are the lines alike?

    _____

    _____

12. How are they different?

    _____

    _____

13. Adding to *x* does what to the line?

    _____

14. Multiplying *x* does what to the line?

    _____

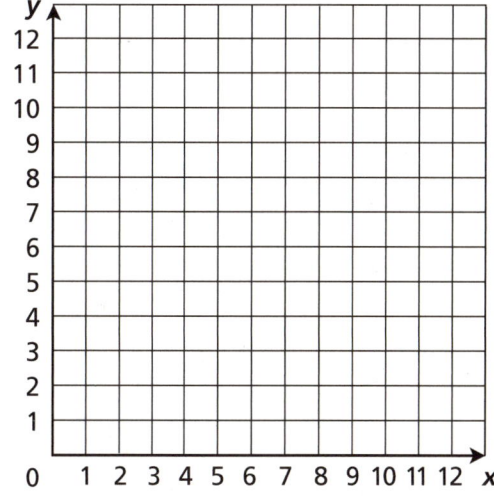

▶ Use a Graph to Solve a Problem

Dorothy collected 30 mL of water from a leaking faucet in 2 hours. She wondered about how long it would take to collect 100 mL of water.

1. Complete the table below to show how much water is collected in 0, 2, and 4 hours.

Time (hr)	0	2	4
Volume of water (mL)	___	___	___

2. Graph the points in the table and extend the line. Use the graph to answer the rest of the questions.

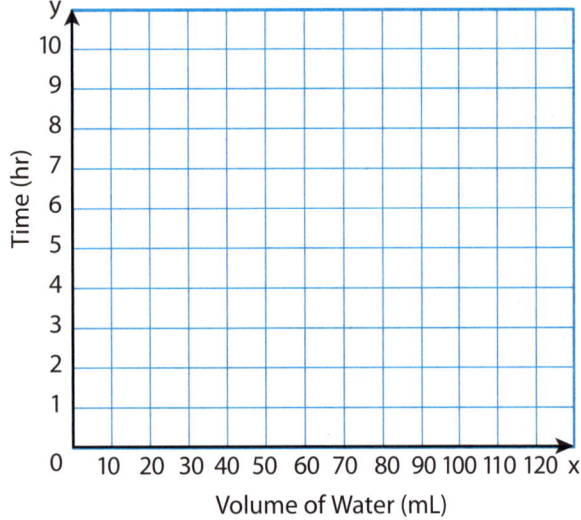

3. How long will it take to collect 90 mL of water?

   _____

4. How much water will collect in 8 hours?

   _____

5. About how long will it take to collect 100 mL of water?

   _____

334 UNIT D LESSON 3 CA Standards: KEY AF 1.4, KEY AF 1.5; AF 1.1 Graph Functions

▶ Negative Numbers in the Real World

A **negative number** is a number that is less than 0, for example, −1, −2, −3, −4, −5, and so on.

1. List real-world situations in which negative numbers are used.

    _____
    _____
    _____

▶ Compare Positive and Negative Numbers

A number line can be extended to include negative numbers. These number lines include positive numbers, negative numbers, and 0.

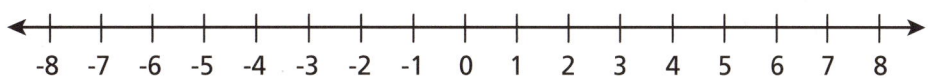

On a number line, the number farther to the right is the greater number.

Compare the following numbers on a number line.
Write >, <, or =.

2. 5 ◯ 8   3. −2 ◯ −6   4. 3 ◯ −3   5. −1 ◯ 0

6. −6 ◯ 7   7. 1 ◯ −4   8. −8 ◯ −7   9. 0 ◯ −5

Write the numbers in order from greatest to least.

10. 4, −7, −5, 2 _____

11. −1, 3, −6, −2 _____

12. Discuss patterns you see in comparing positive and negative numbers, just positive numbers, and just negative numbers.

Class Activity

Vocabulary
origin

▶ Graph Points With Positive and Negative Coordinates

12. Using your ruler, draw a square that has the **origin** (0, 0) as its center. Write an ordered pair to describe the location of each vertex of your square. _____

13. Plot a point at (0, −8). Name two points on the x-axis that will form an isosceles triangle with (0, −8). _____

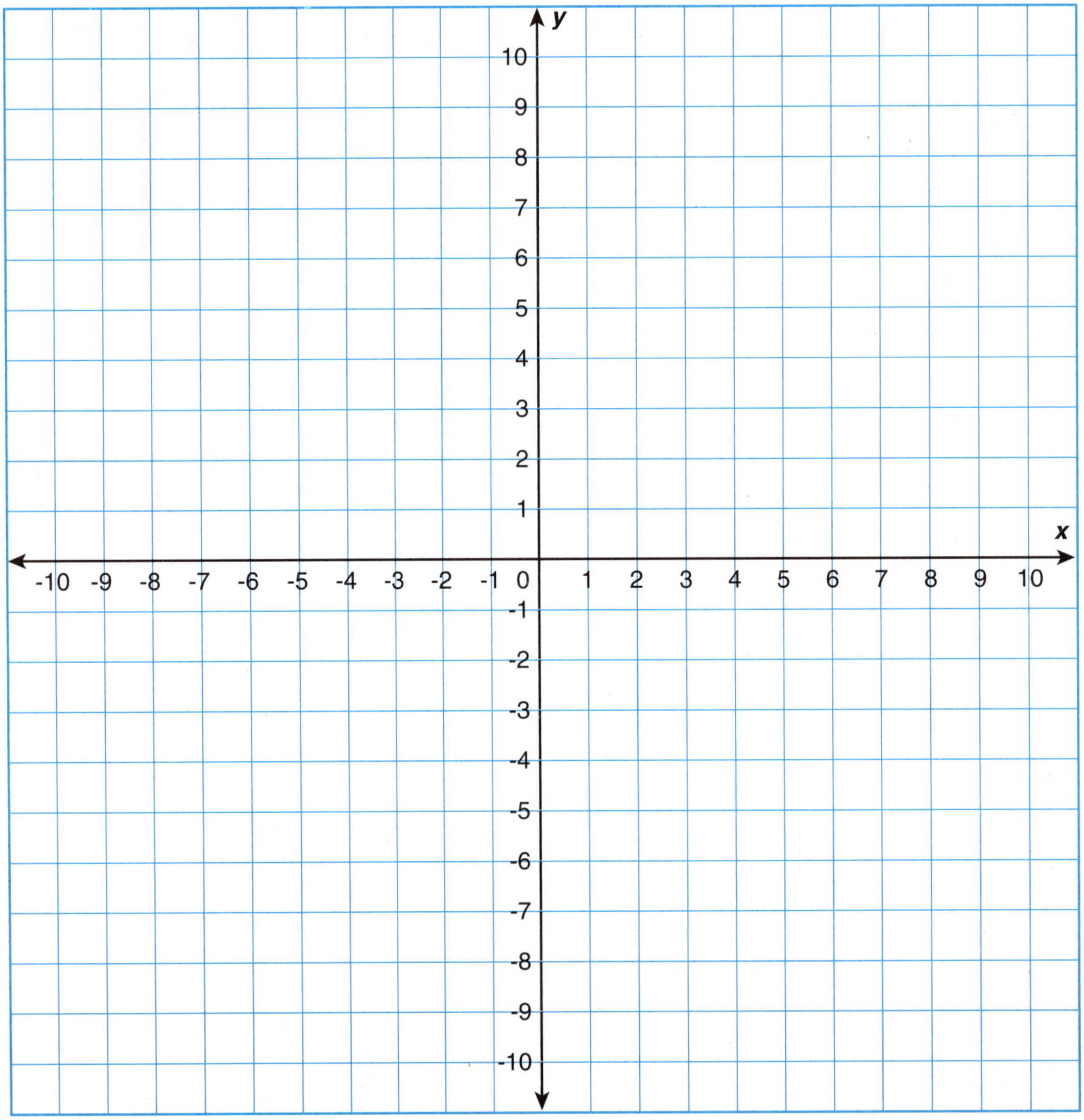

Name _____ Date _____

1.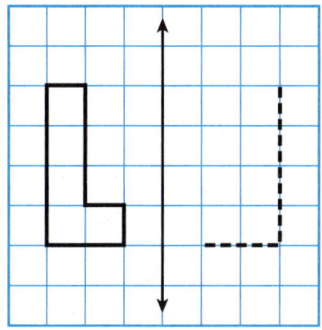
Reflect over the line.

2.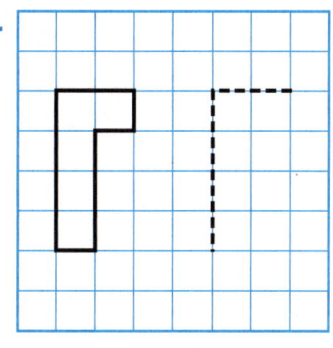
Translate 4 units to the right.

3.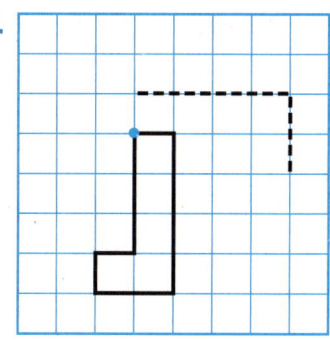
Rotate about the blue point 90° counterclockwise.

4. What are the coordinates of point A?

   _____

5. The coordinates of point B are (5, 6). Draw and label point B.

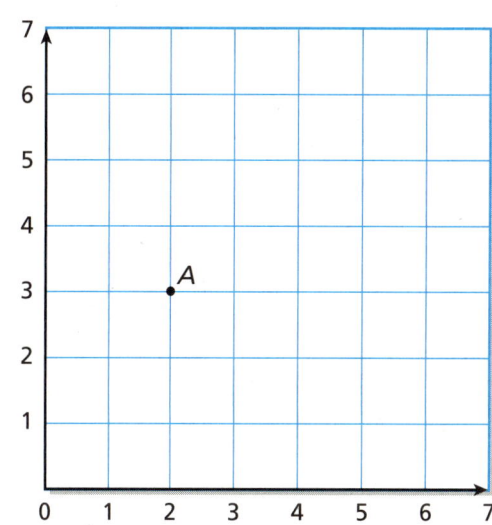

6. The function table at the right shows values for the function $y = 4x$. Write a verbal rule for the function $y = 4x$.

   _____

   _____

Write 3 ordered pairs for the function $y = 4x$.

   _____ _____ _____

$y = 4x$	
x	y
0	0
1	4
2	8
4	16
8	32

UNIT D TEST

7. Complete the table of ordered pairs.

y = x + 7	
x	y
1	
	9
	10
4	

8. Plot the ordered pairs from the table in exercise 7. Draw a line segment through the points.

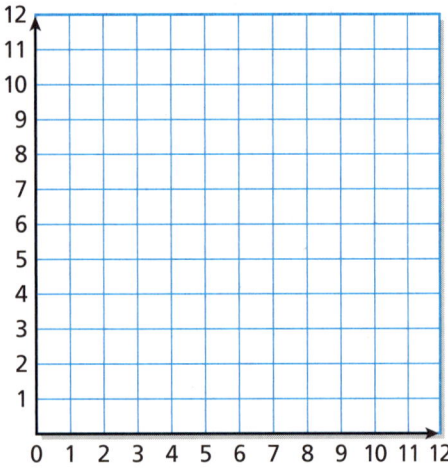

9. Draw the next figure in the pattern.

10. **Extended Response** Describe the pattern in exercise 9. Explain how to find the 16th figure in the pattern.

_____
_____
_____
_____

5-1 Class Activity

▶ Fractional Multiplication

Complete.

1. A racetrack is 8 kilometers long. Alex ran around the track 4 times.

    8 taken 4 times = _____ kilometers

    4 × 8 = _____ kilometers

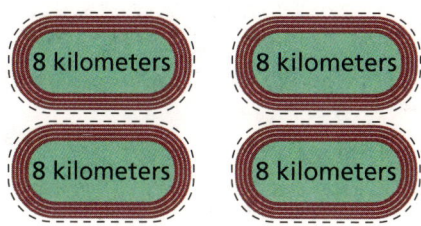

2. Kento ran around the same track $\frac{1}{4}$ times.

    8 taken $\frac{1}{4}$ times = _____ kilometers

    $\frac{1}{4}$ × 8 = _____ kilometers

3. Markers come in sets of 6. Alta has 3 sets.

    6 taken 3 times = _____ markers

    3 × 6 = _____ markers

3 sets of 6

4. Isabel has $\frac{1}{3}$ of a set of 6 markers.

    6 taken $\frac{1}{3}$ times = _____ markers

    $\frac{1}{3}$ × 6 = _____ markers

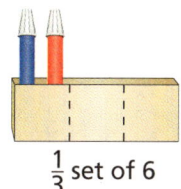

$\frac{1}{3}$ set of 6

▶ Relate Fractional Multiplication and Whole-Number Division

Complete each equation chain like the one shown.

$\frac{1}{4}$ of 8 = $\frac{1}{4}$ × 8 = 8 ÷ 4 = $\frac{8}{4}$ = 2

5. $\frac{1}{3}$ of 9 = _____ = _____ = _____ = _____

6. $\frac{1}{7}$ of 21 = _____ = _____ = _____ = _____

7. $\frac{1}{5}$ of 30 = _____ = _____ = _____ = _____

8. Circle the expression that does *not* mean the same as the others.

    $\frac{1}{6}$ × 24   24 ÷ 6 $\frac{24}{6}$ $\frac{6}{24}$ $\frac{1}{6}$ of 24

UNIT 5 LESSON 1   CA Standards: NS 2.4, 2.5; MR 2.0   Basic Multiplication Concepts **339**

▶ Practice With Unit Fractions

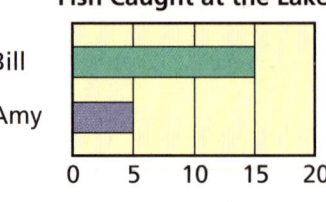

Fish Caught at the Lake

9. How many times as many fish did Bill catch as Amy?
_____

10. How many times as many fish did Amy catch as Bill?
_____

11. What is $\frac{1}{3} \times 15$? What is $15 \div 3$? What is $\frac{15}{3}$?
_____

Write two statements for each pair of players.

12. Compare Gina's points and Brent's points.
_____
_____

13. Compare Brent's points and Jacob's points.
_____
_____

14. Compare Jacob's points and Gina's points.
_____
_____

Points at the Basketball Game

Player	Points
Gina	32
Brent	8
Jacob	4

15. Which are the shortest and longest snakes? How do you know?
_____
_____

16. If Speedy is 25 inches long, how long is Lola?
_____

17. If Pretzel is 50 inches long, how long is Speedy? How long is Lola?
_____

Length of Snakes at the Zoo

Snake	Inches
Speedy	n
Lola	$\frac{1}{5} \times n$
Pretzel	$5 \times n$

Dear Family,

In this unit of *Math Expressions*, your child is studying multiplication and division with fractions.

Multiplication tells how many times we are taking a number. For example, when we take $\frac{4}{5}$ of something, we multiply it by $\frac{4}{5}$ to find the answer. In this unit, your child will learn to:

- multiply a whole number by a unit fraction

  $\frac{1}{b} \times w = \frac{w}{b}$ $\frac{1}{3} \times 5 = \frac{5}{3}$

- multiply a whole number by a non-unit fraction

  $\frac{a}{b} \times w = \frac{a \times w}{b}$ $\frac{2}{3} \times 5 = \frac{10}{3}$

- multiply two fractions

  $\frac{a}{b} \times \frac{c}{d} = \frac{a \times c}{b \times d}$ $\frac{2}{3} \times \frac{5}{7} = \frac{10}{21}$

Division tells us how many of a certain number are inside another number. For example, when we ask how many times $\frac{4}{5}$ fits inside a number, we divide it by $\frac{4}{5}$ to find out. Using the relationship between multiplication and division, your child will discover how to:

- divide a whole number by a unit fraction

  $w \div \frac{1}{d} = w \times d$ $6 \div \frac{1}{5} = 6 \times 5 = 30$

- divide a fraction by a fraction

  $\frac{a}{b} \div \frac{c}{d} = \frac{a}{b} \times \frac{d}{c}$ $\frac{4}{7} \div \frac{3}{5} = \frac{4}{7} \times \frac{5}{3} = \frac{20}{21}$

Throughout the unit, students will also practice the fractional operations they have learned previously—comparing, adding, and subtracting. This helps them maintain what they have learned. It also helps them to see how the various fractional operations are alike and how they are different. It is particularly important for your child to realize that comparing, adding, and subtracting fractions require the denominators to be the same. For multiplying and dividing this is not true.

If you have any questions about this unit, please call or write to me.

Sincerely,
Your child's teacher

Estimada familia:

En esta unidad de *Math Expressions* su niño está estudiando la multiplicación y la división con fracciones.

La multiplicación nos dice cuántas veces se toma un número. Por ejemplo, cuando tomamos $\frac{4}{5}$ de algo, lo multiplicamos por $\frac{4}{5}$ para hallar la respuesta. En esta unidad su niño aprenderá a:

- multiplicar un número entero por una fracción cuyo numerador es uno

    $\boxed{\dfrac{1}{b} \times w = \dfrac{w}{b}}$ $\boxed{\dfrac{1}{3} \times 5 = \dfrac{5}{3}}$

- multiplicar un número entero por una fracción cuyo numerador es diferente de uno

    $\boxed{\dfrac{a}{b} \times w = \dfrac{a \times w}{b}}$ $\boxed{\dfrac{2}{3} \times 5 = \dfrac{10}{3}}$

- multiplicar dos fracciones

    $\boxed{\dfrac{a}{b} \times \dfrac{c}{d} = \dfrac{a \times c}{b \times d}}$ $\boxed{\dfrac{2}{3} \times \dfrac{5}{7} = \dfrac{10}{21}}$

La división nos dice qué cantidad de cierto número está dentro de otro número. Por ejemplo, cuando preguntamos cuántas veces cabe $\frac{4}{5}$ en un número, dividimos el número entre $\frac{4}{5}$ para saberlo. Al usar la relación entre la multiplicación y la división, su niño va a descubrir cómo:

- se divide un número entero por una fracción cuyo numerador es uno

    $\boxed{w \div \dfrac{1}{d} = w \times d}$ $\boxed{6 \div \dfrac{1}{5} = 6 \times 5 = 30}$

- se divide una fracción entre una fracción

    $\boxed{\dfrac{a}{b} \div \dfrac{c}{d} = \dfrac{a}{b} \times \dfrac{d}{c}}$ $\boxed{\dfrac{4}{7} \div \dfrac{3}{5} = \dfrac{4}{7} \times \dfrac{5}{3} = \dfrac{20}{21}}$

En esta unidad los estudiantes también practicarán las operaciones con fracciones que han aprendido anteriormente: comparaciones, sumas y restas. Esto los ayudará a retener lo que han aprendido. También los ayuda a ver en qué se parecen y en qué se diferencian las operaciones con fracciones. Es importante que su niño se dé cuenta de que para comparar, sumar y restar fracciones, las fracciones deben tener el mismo denominador. En la multiplicación y división esto no se aplica.

Si tiene alguna duda o comentario, por favor comuníquese conmigo.

Atentamente,
El maestro de su niño

Visualize the Separate Steps

Silver City is 24 miles away. Gus has driven $\frac{1}{4}$ of the distance. Emma has driven $\frac{3}{4}$ of the distance.

1. How many miles has Gus driven? _____

2. How many miles has Emma driven? _____

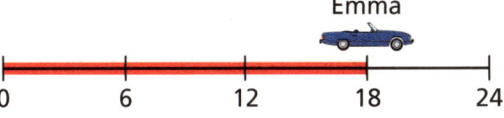

3. How many times as far as Gus has Emma driven? _____

4. If $\frac{1}{5}$ of a distance is 3 km, how far is $\frac{4}{5}$? _____

5. If $\frac{1}{8}$ of a container weighs 2 lbs, how many pounds is $\frac{3}{8}$ of the container? _____

6. If $\frac{1}{7}$ of a book is 4 pages, how many pages is $\frac{2}{7}$ of the book? _____

Shady Grove is 40 miles away. Middletown is $\frac{1}{5}$ of the way there and Parkview is $\frac{2}{5}$ of the way.

7. How many miles away is Middletown? _____

8. How many miles away is Parkview? _____

9. Ocean City is 42 miles from home. We have gone 35 miles. What fraction of the distance have we gone? _____

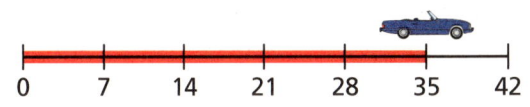

10. Eagle Rock is 72 miles away. When we had gone $\frac{2}{9}$ of the distance, we stopped for gas. How many miles had we traveled? _____

11. Perilous Peak is 80 miles away. We are $\frac{3}{10}$ of the way there. How many more miles do we have to go? _____

12. Windy Bay is 48 miles away. Make up your own fraction word problem with multiplication. Be sure to include a non-unit fraction.

_____

_____

UNIT 5 LESSON 2 — CA Standards: NS 2.5; MR 2.3 — Multiplication With Non-Unit Fractions

5-2 Class Activity

▶ Practice Multiplication With Fractions

Solve the problem pairs.

13. $\frac{1}{3}$ of 18 = _____

    $\frac{2}{3}$ of 18 = _____

14. $\frac{1}{4} \times 32$ = _____

    $\frac{3}{4} \times 32$ = _____

15. $\frac{1}{9} \times 27$ = _____

    $\frac{4}{9} \times 27$ = _____

16. $\frac{1}{6} \times 42$ = _____

    $\frac{5}{6} \times 42$ = _____

17. Circle the one that does *not* mean the same as the others.

    $\frac{2}{3} \times 21$ $\frac{2}{3}$ of 21 $(\frac{1}{3}$ of 21$) + (\frac{1}{3}$ of 21$)$

    $\frac{2}{3} + 21$ $\frac{21}{3} + \frac{21}{3}$ $(\frac{1}{3}$ of 21$) \times 2$

Use the table to answer each question.

18. Which building is the tallest? Which is the shortest? How do you know?

    _____

    _____

    _____

Building	Number of Stories
Bank	n
Bus station	$\frac{1}{6} \times n$
Sport shop	$\frac{5}{6} \times n$
Hotel	$6 \times n$

Suppose the bus station is 2 stories tall.

19. How many stories does the sport shop have? _____

20. How many stories does the bank have? _____

Suppose the bank is 5 stories tall.

21. How many stories tall is the hotel? _____

Suppose the hotel is 36 stories tall.

22. How many stories does the bank have? _____

23. How many stories does the bus station have? _____

24. How many stories does the sport shop have? _____

▶ Visualize Fractional Answers

Farmer Hanson, Farmer Diaz, and Farmer Smith each have 3 acres of land. They each plowed $\frac{1}{5}$ of their land.

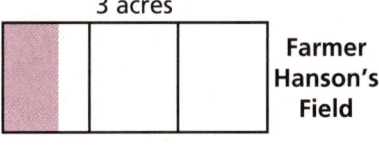

1. Can we tell from the picture how many acres Farmer Hanson plowed? Why or why not?

   _____

   _____

2. Farmer Smith plowed $\frac{1}{5}$ of each acre. Can we tell from the picture how many acres she plowed? Explain.

   _____

   _____

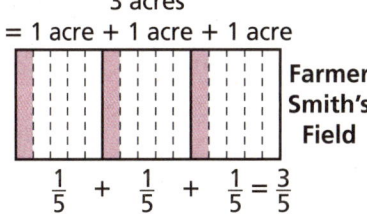

3. How can we tell from Farmer Diaz's field that $\frac{1}{5}$ of each acre added together is the same as $\frac{1}{5}$ of the whole field?

   _____

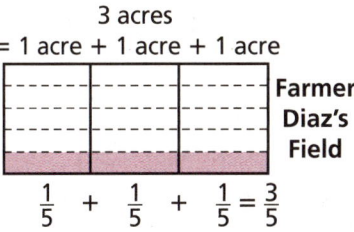

4. Why is $\frac{1}{5}$ of 3 acres the same as $3 \times \frac{1}{5}$?

   _____

   _____

5. Farmer Belinsky has 7 acres of land. He plowed $\frac{1}{8}$ of each acre. How many acres did he plow altogether?

   _____

6. Farmer Davis has 4 acres of land. He plowed $\frac{1}{3}$ of the field. How many acres did he plow?

   _____

Solve.

Show your work.

7. Tess practices the flute $\frac{1}{6}$ hour each day. This week she practiced 5 days. How many hours did she practice this week?

   _____

UNIT 5 LESSON 3   CA Standards: NS 2.4, 2.5; MR 2.3   Multiplication With Fractional Solutions **345**

Class Activity

Name _____ **Date** _____

▶ Multiply by a Non-Unit Fraction

8. Circle the one that does not mean the same as the others.

   $\frac{1}{4}$ of 3 $\frac{1}{4} \times 3$ $4 \times \frac{1}{3}$ $\frac{1}{4} + \frac{1}{4} + \frac{1}{4}$ $3 \times \frac{1}{4}$

Circle the fractions on the number lines to help you multiply.

9. $\frac{1}{7} \times 2 =$ _____

10. $\frac{3}{7} \times 2 =$ _____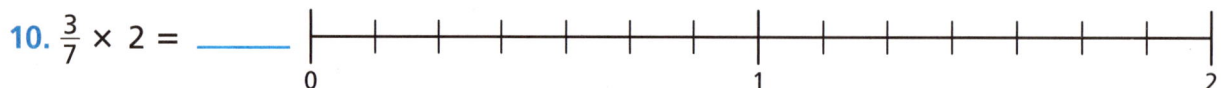

11. $\frac{1}{5} \times 3 =$ _____

12. $\frac{4}{5} \times 3 =$ _____

13. $\frac{1}{6} \times 4 =$ _____

14. $\frac{5}{6} \times 4 =$ _____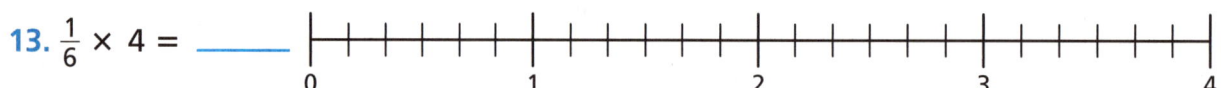

15. $\frac{1}{3} \times 8 =$ _____

16. $\frac{2}{3} \times 8 =$ _____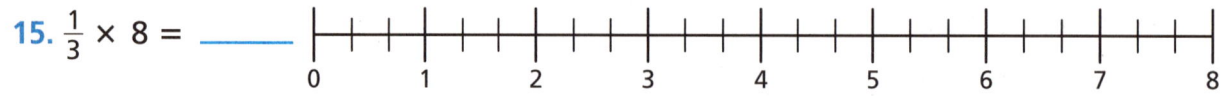

346 UNIT 5 LESSON 3   CA Standards: NS 2.4, 2.5; MR 2.3   Multiplication With Fractional Solutions

5-5 Class Activity

▶ **Simplify and Multiply Fractions**

Multiply. Simplify first if you can.

1. $\frac{2}{3} \times 30 =$ _____

2. $\frac{2}{5} \times 35 =$ _____

3. $\frac{5}{6} \times 4 =$ _____

4. $\frac{7}{16} \times 8 =$ _____

5. $\frac{7}{20} \times \frac{5}{14} =$ _____

6. $\frac{2}{16} \times \frac{4}{21} =$ _____

7. $\frac{9}{10} \times \frac{7}{10} =$ _____

8. $\frac{7}{15} \times \frac{10}{21} =$ _____

9. $\frac{5}{24} \times \frac{6}{25} =$ _____

10. $\frac{5}{8} \times \frac{32}{45} =$ _____

11. $\frac{8}{49} \times \frac{7}{10} =$ _____

12. $\frac{7}{25} \times \frac{3}{4} =$ _____

13. Circle the fraction that does not mean the same as the others.

$\frac{3}{9}$ $\frac{1}{3}$ $\frac{8}{24}$ $\frac{10}{30}$ $\frac{6}{18}$ $\frac{9}{36}$ $\frac{20}{60}$

UNIT 5 LESSON 5   CA Standards: NS 2.5   Multiplication Strategies **347**

5-5 Class Activity

▶ Problem-Solving Situations

Solve.

Show your work.

14. In the Fireside Ski Shop, $\frac{11}{28}$ of the ski caps have tassels. Of the caps with tassels, $\frac{7}{11}$ are blue. What fraction of the caps in the shop are blue with tassels?

_____

15. In the shop, $\frac{27}{32}$ of the jackets have zippers. Of the jackets with zippers, $\frac{8}{9}$ have hoods. What fraction of the jackets in the shop have both zippers and hoods?

_____

16. Five of the 16 workers in the shop know how to ski. $\frac{1}{5}$ of those who can ski know how to snowboard. What fraction of the workers can ski and snowboard?

_____

▶ The Puzzled Penguin

Dear Math Students,

I have a string that is $\frac{3}{4}$ of a yard long. I need to take $\frac{7}{12}$ of it. You can see how I solved the problem at the right.

$$\frac{7}{12} \times \frac{3}{4} = \frac{7 \times 3}{12 \times 4} = \frac{21}{3} = 7 \text{ yd}$$
$$3 \times 1$$

I simplified by changing 12 × 4 to 3 × 1.

Now I'm wondering about my answer. When you take a fraction of a fraction, you should get a smaller fraction. But my answer is larger. What mistake did I make? How do I correct it?

Thank you.
Puzzled Penguin

17. Write a response to the Puzzled Penguin.

_____
_____
_____
_____

348 UNIT 5 LESSON 5   CA Standards: NS 2.4, 2.5; MR 3.2   Multiplication Strategies

Class Activity 5-6

▶ Compare Multiplication and Addition

These fraction strips show how we add and multiply fractions.

Add: $\frac{3}{5} + \frac{2}{5} = \frac{5}{5}$

Multiply: Take $\frac{2}{5}$ of the whole. Then take $\frac{3}{5}$ of each fifth. $\frac{3}{5} \times \frac{2}{5} = \frac{6}{25}$

1. Which problem above has the greater answer? How do you know?

   _____

2. Tell which of these questions will have the greater answer. Solve each one.

   $\frac{3}{7} + \frac{2}{7} =$ _____ $\frac{3}{7} \times \frac{2}{7} =$ _____

   _____

3. If the denominators are different, can you still tell which answer will be greater? Circle your answer, then solve to check.   **yes**   **no**

   $\frac{3}{4} + \frac{1}{6} =$ _____ $\frac{3}{4} \times \frac{1}{6} =$ _____

▶ Compare Fractional and Whole-Number Operations

Circle each expression with an answer less than the first number. Put a box around each with an answer greater than the first number.

4. $a + b$	5. $a - b$	6. $a \times b$	
7. $\frac{a}{b} + \frac{c}{d}$	8. $\frac{a}{b} - \frac{c}{d}$	9. $\frac{a}{b} \times \frac{c}{d}$	

> a and b are whole numbers greater than 1.
>
> All of the fractions are less than 1.

10. How is multiplying fractions different from multiplying whole numbers?

    _____

    _____

UNIT 5 LESSON 6   CA Standards: KEY NS 2.3; NS 2.4; MR 3.3   Relate Fractional Operations **349**

5-6 Class Activity

Vocabulary
commutative property

▶ Word Problems With Mixed Operations

Amber, a very fit snail, moved $\frac{7}{9}$ yard in an hour. She challenged the other snails to try to do better.

Write how far each snail went. Show your work.

11. Willy moved $\frac{4}{5}$ as far as Amber. _____

12. Dusty went $\frac{1}{3}$ of a yard less than Amber. _____

13. Pearl went twice as far as Amber. _____

14. Casey moved $\frac{4}{9}$ of a yard more than Amber. _____

15. Minnie moved half as far as Amber. _____

16. Make up your own question about another snail, Shelly. Ask a classmate to solve it.

_____

_____

▶ The Commutative Property and Fractions

$\frac{a}{b} \times \frac{c}{d} = \frac{c}{d} \times \frac{a}{b}$ This relationship is known as the **commutative property**. Look at the proof below.

$$\frac{a}{b} \times \frac{c}{d} \;=\; \frac{a \times c}{b \times d} \;=\; \frac{c \times a}{d \times b} \;=\; \frac{c}{d} \times \frac{a}{b}$$

Problem   Step 1   Step 2   Step 3

17. Explain why each step is true.

Step 1 _____

_____

Step 2 _____

_____

Step 3 _____

_____

350 UNIT 5 LESSON 6   CA Standards: NS 2.5; AF 1.1; MR 2.3   Relate Fractional Operations

Name _____ **Date** _____

▶ Investigate Decimal Patterns

These number lines show decimal equivalents for some common fractions. Discuss patterns you see.

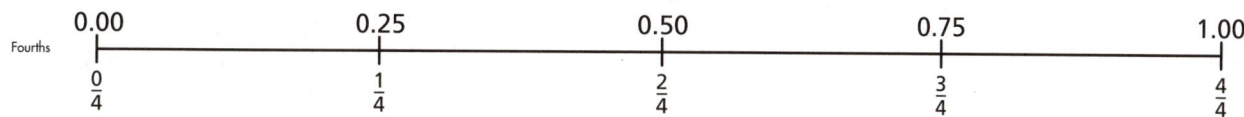

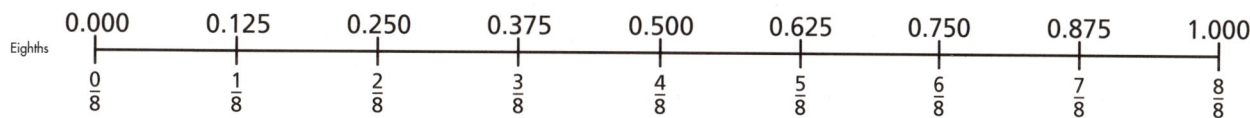

Fourths, Eighths, Fifths, Thirds, Sixths

UNIT 5 LESSON 7   CA Standards: KEY NS 1.2; KEY NS 1.5   Find Decimal Equivalents of Fractions **351**

Problems With Fractions and Decimals

Some problems use both fractions and decimals. Converting the fractions to decimals can sometimes make it easier to compare or work with the numbers.

Solve.

Show your work.

1. Malcolm made $\frac{2}{7}$ of his free throws this year. His friend Darius made 0.31 of his free throws. Who has a better free-throw record this year?

   _____

2. Zoe made $1,000 last year and saved $\frac{7}{8}$ of it. This year she also made $1,000 and saved $890. How much more did she save this year?

   _____

3. Berta needs $\frac{7}{8}$ of a pint of whipped cream to make a dessert. She has 0.9 of a pint. How much whipped cream will be left over?

   _____

4. The bolts that hold the cables on Trudi's bike measure about 0.12 inches across. She has a set of wrenches in these sizes, measured in fractions of an inch: $\frac{5}{32}, \frac{1}{8}, \frac{3}{16}, \frac{1}{4}, \frac{3}{32}$.

   Which wrench should she use?

   _____

5. Trudi also needs to tighten the axle bolts, which measure 0.4 inches across. Does she have a wrench large enough?

   _____

5-8 Class Activity

▶ Explore Fractional Shares

There are 4 people in the Walton family, but there are only 3 waffles. How can the Waltons share the waffles equally?

Divide each waffle into 4 pieces.

Each person's share of one waffle is $\frac{1}{4}$. Since there are 3 waffles, each person gets 3 of the $\frac{1}{4}$s, or $\frac{3}{4}$ of a waffle.

$3 \div 4 = 3 \times \frac{1}{4} = \frac{3}{4}$

1. Suppose there are 5 people and 4 waffles.

   What is each person's share of 1 waffle? _____

   What is each person's share of 4 waffles? _____

   Complete the equation: $4 \div 5 =$ _____ × _____ = _____

2. Suppose there are 10 people and 7 waffles.

   What is each person's share of 1 waffle? _____

   What is each person's share of 7 waffles? _____

   Complete the equation: $7 \div 10 =$ _____ × _____ = _____

Complete.

3. $5 \div 6 =$ _____ × _____ = _____

4. $4 \div 9 =$ _____ × _____ = _____

Give your answer in the format of an equation.

5. How can you divide 7 waffles equally among 8 people?

   _____

6. How can you divide 39 waffles equally among 5 serving plates?

   _____

7. Discuss why these equations are true for any whole numbers n and d.

   $n \div d = \underbrace{n \times \frac{1}{d}}_{n \text{ unit fractions } \frac{1}{d}} = \frac{n}{d}$

UNIT 5 LESSON 8   CA Standards: NS 2.4, 2.5   When Dividing Is Also Multiplying **353**

5-8 Class Activity

▶ Divide by a Unit Fraction

8. How many $\frac{1}{8}$s are there in 1? Write a division equation to show this.

_____

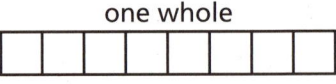
one whole

9. How many $\frac{1}{8}$s are there in 3? Write a division equation to show this.

_____

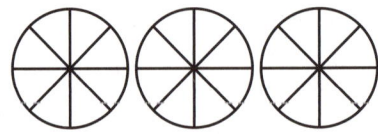

10. Why can you also use the multiplication equation $3 \times 8 = 24$ to show how many $\frac{1}{8}$s are in 3?

_____

11. How many $\frac{1}{4}$s are there in 5? Write a division and a multiplication equation to show this.

_____

12. Complete the equation. w and d are whole numbers.

$$w \div \frac{1}{d} =$$

Write a division equation. Use multiplication to solve each word problem.

Show your work.

13. Olivia made 9 sandwiches and cut each one into fourths. How many fourths does she have?

_____

14. The 10 members of a hiking club will walk 9 miles. Each person will carry the food pack for an equal distance. How far will each hiker carry the food pack?

_____

15. Damon has a 6-pound bag of cat food. He feeds his cat $\frac{1}{8}$ pound every day. How many days will the bag last?

_____

16. Jodie has a box of 12 chocolates. She and her 7 friends will share them equally. How many chocolates will each person get? Give your answer as a simplified mixed number.

_____

When Dividing Is Also Multiplying

5–9 Class Activity

▶ **Add, Subtract, Compare, and Multiply Fractions**

	$\frac{1}{3}$ and $\frac{1}{6}$
>	$\frac{1}{3} > \frac{1}{6}$ or $\frac{2}{6} > \frac{1}{6}$
+	$\frac{1}{3} + \frac{1}{6} = \frac{2}{6} + \frac{1}{6} = \frac{3}{6} = \frac{1}{2}$
−	$\frac{1}{3} - \frac{1}{6} = \frac{2}{6} - \frac{1}{6} = \frac{1}{6}$
×	$\frac{1}{3} \times \frac{1}{6} = \frac{1}{18}$

The fraction box to the right shows the same two fractions compared, added, subtracted, and multiplied.

Complete the fraction box.

1.

	$\frac{2}{5}$ and $\frac{7}{10}$
>	
+	
−	
×	

2.

	$\frac{3}{5}$ and $\frac{4}{7}$
>	
+	
−	
×	

3. How are adding, subtracting, and comparing fractions alike?
_____

4. How is multiplication different from the other operations?
_____

Dear Math Students,

One of my friends said that he would give $\frac{1}{2}$ of his sandwich to me and $\frac{1}{2}$ of his sandwich to my sister. My sister said, "But then you won't have any left for yourself." This doesn't make sense to me. I know that $\frac{1}{2} + \frac{1}{2} = \frac{2}{4}$. My friend should have plenty left for himself. Did I do something wrong? What do you think?

Puzzled Penguin

5. Write a response to the Puzzled Penguin.
_____
_____
_____

Class Activity

▶ Word Problems With Mixed Operations

Solve. Answer first in unsimplified form and then in the simplest form.

6. Yesterday Mr. Swenson made $2\frac{3}{4}$ quarts of strawberry jam and $1\frac{1}{8}$ quarts of raspberry jam. How much more strawberry jam did he make than raspberry?

   _____

7. Today Mr. Swenson is making $\frac{2}{5}$ of a quart of grape jelly. He will give $\frac{1}{2}$ of this amount to his neighbor. How many quarts will the neighbor get?

   _____

8. Mr. Swenson is also making $2\frac{1}{6}$ quarts of cherry jelly and $3\frac{1}{12}$ quarts of orange jelly. He will mix the two kinds together. How much of this mixed jelly will he have?

   _____

9. Yesterday Mr. Swenson made $\frac{7}{10}$ of a quart of blueberry jam. His family ate $\frac{1}{10}$ of it. How much of the blueberry jam is left?

   _____

10. Suppose Mr. Swenson has jars that hold $\frac{5}{6}$ of a quart, jars that hold $\frac{3}{4}$ of a quart, and jars that hold $\frac{2}{3}$ of a quart. Which size holds the most? Which size holds the least? How do you know?

    _____

    _____

11. Suppose Mr. Swenson has jars in these sizes:
    $\frac{3}{4}$ quart, $\frac{2}{5}$ quart, $\frac{5}{8}$ quart, $\frac{4}{5}$ quart, $\frac{3}{10}$ quart

    Give the size of these jars in decimal numbers.

    _____

Divide a Whole Number by a Fraction

Solve. Use the number lines to help you.

A mountain trail is 6 miles long. A group of runners will race to the top of the mountain.

1. The runners expect to see a marker every $\frac{1}{4}$ mile. How many markers will they see? Write the division equation and the answer.

   Think: How many $\frac{1}{4}$s are there in 6? Look at the number line.

   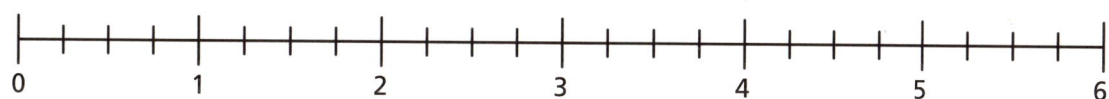

2. The runners expect a water station every $\frac{3}{4}$ mile. Write the division equation and the answer. How many water stations will there be?

   Think: How many $\frac{3}{4}$s are there in 6? Use the number line.

   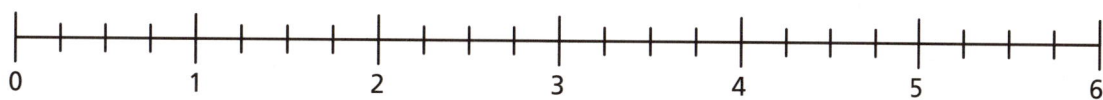

3. How many times as great is your first answer as your second answer? Explain why.

4. Explain why you can solve $6 \div \frac{3}{4}$ in two steps: $6 * 4 = 24$ and then $24 \div 3 = 8$.

5-10 Class Activity

▶ Divide a Fraction by a Fraction

Solve.

5. Alison has $\frac{2}{3}$ of an hour to write postcards. It takes her $\frac{1}{6}$ of an hour to write each one. How many can she write? Write the division equation and the answer.

   Think: How many $\frac{1}{6}$s are in $\frac{2}{3}$? Use the number line.

_____

▶ Solve Multiplication Equations

Find the unknown factor. Rewrite the equation as a division.

Division Equation

6. $\frac{2}{3} \times$ _____ $= \frac{8}{15}$ $\frac{8}{15} \div \frac{2}{3} =$ _____

7. $\frac{5}{7} \times$ _____ $= \frac{15}{56}$ _____

8. $\frac{5}{6} \times$ _____ $= \frac{15}{24}$ _____

9. $\frac{2}{5} \times$ _____ $= \frac{6}{20}$ _____

10. $\frac{5}{8} \times$ _____ $= \frac{20}{72}$ _____

These products have been simplified. Use the unsimplified fraction to divide.

11. $\frac{2}{5} \times$ _____ $= \frac{6}{20} = \frac{3}{10}$ _____

12. $\frac{3}{4} \times$ _____ $= \frac{15}{24} = \frac{5}{8}$ _____

358 UNIT 5 LESSON 10   CA Standards: KEY NS 1.5; NS 2.5   Explore Fractional Division

▶ Unsimplify to Make the Product Divisible

$\frac{2}{3} \div \frac{5}{7} = ?$ We cannot divide the top by 5 or the bottom by 7.

We need to unsimplify $\frac{2}{3}$ so we can divide: $\frac{2}{3} \times \left(\frac{5}{5} \times \frac{7}{7} \right)$

1. Why do you multiply by $\frac{5}{5}$ and $\frac{7}{7}$?

   _____

   _____

   _____

   Now let's divide: $\frac{2 \times 5 \times 7}{3 \times 5 \times 7} \div \frac{5}{7} = \frac{(2 \times 5 \times 7) \div 5}{(3 \times 5 \times 7) \div 7}$

2. In the numerator, $5 \div 5 = 1$.
   Divide and write the simplified numerator: _____

3. In the denominator, $7 \div 7 = 1$.
   Divide and write the simplified denominator: _____

4. Complete the new equation. $\frac{2 \times \underline{\qquad}}{3 \times \underline{\qquad}} = \frac{\underline{\quad}}{\underline{\quad}}$

5. What happened to the divisor $\frac{5}{7}$ in step 4?

   _____

Unsimplify the product to complete each division.

6. $\frac{3}{8} \div \frac{2}{5} = \underline{\qquad\qquad} \quad \frac{\underline{\quad}}{\underline{\quad}} = \frac{\underline{\quad}}{\underline{\quad}}$

7. $\frac{4}{9} \div \frac{3}{8} = \underline{\qquad\qquad} \quad \frac{\underline{\quad}}{\underline{\quad}} = \frac{\underline{\quad}}{\underline{\quad}} = \frac{\underline{\quad}}{\underline{\quad}}$

8. $\frac{2}{9} \div \frac{3}{10} = \underline{\qquad\qquad} \quad \frac{\underline{\quad}}{\underline{\quad}} = \frac{\underline{\quad}}{\underline{\quad}}$

9. $\frac{2}{7} \div \frac{4}{3} = \underline{\qquad\qquad} \quad \frac{\underline{\quad}}{\underline{\quad}} = \frac{\underline{\quad}}{\underline{\quad}} = \frac{\underline{\quad}}{\underline{\quad}}$

5–11 Class Activity

▶ Understand Division by Inversion

You can unsimplify and divide in one step.

Unsimplify and divide.   Multiply

$$\frac{2}{3} \div \frac{5}{7} = \frac{2 \times 5 \times 7}{3 \times 5 \times 7} \div \frac{5}{7} = \frac{2}{3} \times \frac{7}{5} = \frac{14}{15}$$

10. How is the final multiplication related to the original division?

_____

_____

11. Complete the algebra equation.

$\frac{a}{b} \div \frac{c}{d} = \frac{}{} \times \frac{}{}$

12. Use the algebra equation to help you divide.

$\frac{4}{9} \div \frac{3}{5} =$ _____

13. Solve the equation by unsimplifying the factor.

$\frac{4}{9} \div \frac{3}{5} =$ _____

14. What do you notice about the answers to exercises 12 and 13?

_____

▶ Practice Fractional Division

Complete these fractional divisions using any method.

15. $\frac{1}{10} \div \frac{2}{3} =$ _____   **16.** $\frac{5}{12} \div \frac{5}{6} =$ _____

17. $\frac{2}{9} \div \frac{3}{4} =$ _____   **18.** $2\frac{1}{4} \div \frac{3}{4} =$ _____

19. $\frac{15}{16} \div \frac{5}{4} =$ _____   **20.** $\frac{15}{32} \div \frac{3}{4} =$ _____

5-12 Class Activity

▶ Solve Fraction Word Problems

The Skyline Skateboard Factory times its workers to see how fast they work. The table shows the time it takes each worker at the factory to make one skateboard. Use the table to solve each problem.

Worker	Time
Kristy	$\frac{3}{5}$ hours
Arturo	$\frac{2}{3}$ hours
Cleta	$\frac{5}{6}$ hours
Tim	$\frac{3}{4}$ hours

1. Tim worked for $3\frac{3}{4}$ hours. How many skateboards did he make?

   _____

2. Today Kristy worked for $3\frac{1}{3}$ hours. How many skateboards and part-skateboards did she make?

   _____

3. Cleta usually works 5 hours a day. How many skateboards and part-skateboards can she make in a day?

   _____

4. Yesterday Arturo worked $5\frac{1}{3}$ hours. How many skateboards and part-skateboards did he make?

   _____

5. Who is the fastest worker at the Skyline Skateboard Factory?

   _____

➡ 6. **On the Back** Write a real-world word problem with a solution that involves dividing $3\frac{1}{3}$ by $\frac{3}{5}$. Solve your problem.

Show your work.

UNIT 5 LESSON 12   CA Standards: NS 2.5; MR 2.0   Investigate Division by Inversion **361**

Name _____ Date _____

Solve Word Problems With Multiplication and Division

Decide whether you need to multiply or divide. Then solve each problem.

1. A turtle crawls $3\frac{1}{3}$ yards in an hour. How far will it crawl in 2 hours?

   _____

   How far will the turtle crawl in $\frac{3}{4}$ of an hour?

   _____

2. Emily has $\frac{3}{5}$ of a ton of sand. She will move it by wheelbarrow to the garden. Her wheelbarrow holds $\frac{1}{10}$ of a ton. How many trips will she make?

   _____

3. Tawanna runs $2\frac{7}{10}$ miles every day. She stops every $\frac{9}{10}$ of a mile to rest. How many stops does she make?

   _____

4. Roberto has a recipe that calls for $\frac{3}{4}$ cup of flour. He wants to use only $\frac{1}{2}$ of the recipe today. How much flour will he need?

   _____

5. A picnic jug holds $\frac{5}{8}$ of a gallon of lemonade. Each paper cup holds $\frac{1}{12}$ of a gallon. How many paper cups, and parts of cups, can be filled?

   _____

6. On the White Gate Chicken Farm $\frac{7}{8}$ of the eggs usually hatch. This year only $\frac{2}{3}$ as many eggs hatched. What fraction of the eggs hatched this year?

   _____

5-13 Class Activity

▶ Compare Fractional and Whole-Number Results

In the equations below, *a* and *b* are whole numbers greater than 1. $\frac{n}{d}$ is a fraction less than 1. Answer the questions about the equations.

Multiplication

7. $a \times b = c$

   Will *c* be greater than or less than *a*? _____ Why?
   _____
   _____

8. $a \times \frac{n}{d} = c$

   Will *c* be greater than or less than *a*? _____ Why?
   _____
   _____

Division

9. $a \div b = c$

   Will *c* be greater than or less than *a*? _____ Why?
   _____
   _____

10. $a \div \frac{n}{d} = c$

    Will *c* be greater than or less than *a*? _____ Why?
    _____
    _____

Circle the greater answer. Do not try to calculate the answer.

11. $4{,}826 \times 581$ $\quad 4{,}826 \div 581$

12. $\frac{27}{83} \times \frac{13}{72}$ $\quad \frac{27}{83} \div \frac{13}{72}$

364 UNIT 5 LESSON 13   CA Standards: NS 2.4; MR 3.0   Distinguish Multiplication From Division

▶ Predict the Size of the Result

Decide what operation to use, predict the size of the result, then solve the problem.

13. Lucy spends 4 hours a week baby-sitting. Her sister Lily spends $\frac{7}{8}$ as much time baby-sitting. Does Lily baby-sit for more or less than 4 hours?

    _____

    Now find the exact amount of time that Lily baby-sits.

    _____

14. Yoshi has a rope 30 feet long. He must cut it into pieces that are each $\frac{5}{6}$ of a foot long. Will he get more or fewer than 30 pieces?

    _____

    Now find the exact number of pieces that Yoshi will get.

    _____

15. Carlos can throw a ball 14 yards. His friend Raul can throw $\frac{3}{7}$ of that distance. Is Raul's throw longer or shorter than 14 yards?

    _____

    Now find the exact length of Raul's throw.

    _____

16. An apple orchard covers 12 acres. There is a watering spout for every $\frac{1}{4}$ of an acre. Are there more or fewer than 12 watering spouts?

    _____

    Now find the exact number of watering spouts in the orchard.

    _____

▶ Summarize Fractional Operations

17. You have just won a prize on a new quiz show called *Quick Thinking*. The prize will be n CDs from your favorite music store. You also have a chance to change your prize if you think you can make it better. The screen shows the other choices that you have. Which one will you choose?

_____

18. Suppose that $n = 6$. How many CDs have you won? _____

19. Suppose that $n = 12$. How many CDs have you won? _____

20. Summarize what you have learned about the size of the answers when you mulitiply and divide by whole numbers and by fractions.

▶ Choose the Operation

Decide what operation to use. Then solve. Simplify your answers.

1. Hala can ride her bike $7\frac{1}{2}$ miles in an hour. How far will she ride in 3 hours? How far will she ride in $\frac{2}{3}$ of an hour?

2. Eryn's pet rabbit eats $\frac{5}{12}$ of a pound of food every day. If Eryn buys rabbit food in 5-pound bags, how often does she buy a new bag of rabbit food?

3. Jason practices the trumpet for $1\frac{2}{3}$ hours every day. He stops every $\frac{1}{3}$ of an hour to rest. How many stops does he make?

4. Jonathan can throw a baseball $10\frac{1}{3}$ yards. His brother Joey can throw a baseball $13\frac{1}{12}$ yards. How much farther can Joey throw the ball?

5. Kim bought $\frac{3}{8}$ of a pound of sunflower seeds and $\frac{3}{16}$ of a pound of thistle seed for her bird feeder. How much seed did she buy in all?

6. Casandra's fish bowl holds $\frac{9}{10}$ of a gallon of water. It is now $\frac{2}{3}$ full. How much water does it have?

▶ Estimate Answers

7. Marcus plays basketball for 9 hours each week. His friend Luis spends $\frac{5}{6}$ as much time playing basketball. Who plays more basketball?

8. How much time does Luis spend playing basketball?

9. Stacey's long jump is 10 feet. That is $\frac{5}{6}$ of a foot longer than Ron's jump. Does Ron jump more or less than 10 feet?

10. How long was Ron's jump?

UNIT 5 LESSON 14 CA Standards: NS 2.5; MR 1.0, 2.0 Review Operations With Fractions **367**

Practice Fractional Operations

Answer in the simplest form.

11. $\frac{7}{15} \div \frac{2}{3} =$ _____

12. $\frac{5}{12} \div \frac{3}{8} =$ _____

13. $\frac{1}{8} + \frac{5}{6} =$ _____

14. $\frac{4}{9} \div 8 =$ _____

15. $\frac{4}{7} - \frac{1}{3} =$ _____

16. $\frac{5}{8} \times \frac{5}{12} =$ _____

17. $\frac{3}{5} - \frac{6}{35} =$ _____

18. $\frac{2}{5} \times 5 =$ _____

19. $\frac{1}{6} + \frac{2}{9} =$ _____

20. $\frac{2}{3} - \frac{1}{12} =$ _____

21. $\frac{7}{8} \times \frac{2}{5} =$ _____

22. $3 - \frac{4}{5} =$ _____

Summarize

a is a whole number greater than 1.

$\frac{n}{d}$ is a fraction less than 1.

Write whether c is greater than (>) or less than (<) a.

23. $a \times \frac{n}{d} = c$ c ◯ a

24. $a \div \frac{n}{d} = c$ c ◯ a

25. $a + \frac{n}{d} = c$ c ◯ a

26. $a - \frac{n}{d} = c$ c ◯ a

U5–Test

Unit Test

Name _____ Date _____

Solve. Show your work.

1. $\frac{1}{5} \times 2 =$ _____

2. $\frac{3}{5} \times 2 =$ _____

3. $\frac{1}{5} \times 20 =$ _____

4. $\frac{2}{3} \times 30 =$ _____

5. $\frac{3}{4} \times \frac{2}{5} =$ _____

6. $\frac{2}{3} \times \frac{6}{10} =$ _____

7. Todd worked in the garden for $\frac{3}{4}$ of an hour. He spent $\frac{1}{4}$ of that time digging weeds. How long did he dig weeds?

_____

Give the decimal equivalent.

8. $\frac{1}{8} =$ _____

9. $\frac{3}{4} =$ _____

Give the fraction equivalent.

10. $0.\overline{3} =$ _____

11. $0.8 =$ _____

12. How is multiplying fractions different from adding and subtracting them?

_____

_____

_____

_____

UNIT 5 TEST

Name _____ Date _____

Solve. Show your work.

13. $3 \div 5 =$ _____

14. $3 \div \frac{1}{5} =$ _____

15. $3 \div \frac{2}{5} =$ _____

16. $\frac{8}{9} \div \frac{2}{3} =$ _____

17. $\frac{3}{7} \div \frac{4}{5} =$ _____

18. $\frac{2}{3} \div \frac{8}{9} =$ _____

19. A picnic jug holds $\frac{7}{8}$ of a gallon of lemonade. The lemonade will be poured into glasses that each hold $\frac{1}{16}$ of a gallon. How many glasses can be filled?

_____

20. **Extended Response** Will $4 \div \frac{2}{3}$ be more or less than 4? Explain why.

_____

_____

_____

_____

370 UNIT 5 TEST

Identify Prisms

Vocabulary
base
prism

Write the shape of the base and use it to name the prism.

1.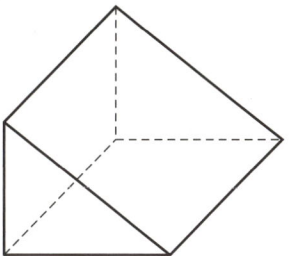

   Base: _____

   Name: _____

2.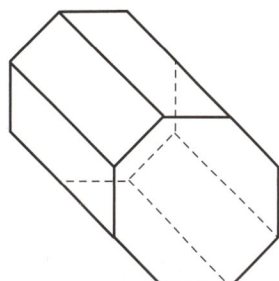

   Base: _____

   Name: _____

3.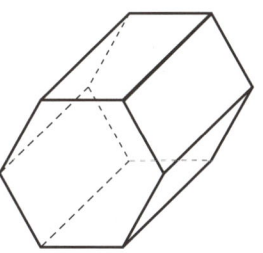

   Base: _____

   Name: _____

4.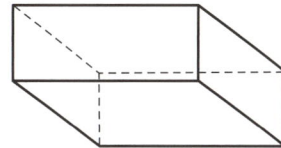

   Base: _____

   Name: _____

5.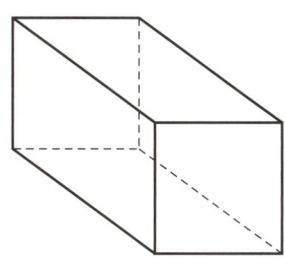

   Base: _____

   Name: _____

6.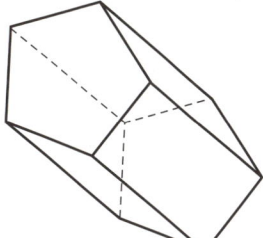

   Base: _____

   Name: _____

UNIT E LESSON 1   CA Standards: MG 2.0   Prisms and Cylinders 371

Name _____ **Date** _____

Vocabulary
cylinder
net
circumference

▶ **Discuss Cylinders**

These are examples of a special kind of solid called a **cylinder**.

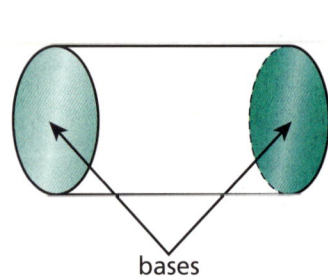
bases

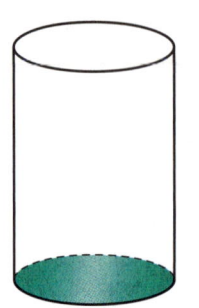

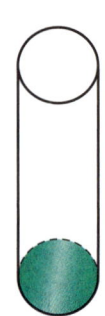

7. List three real-world examples of cylinders.
   _____

8. How is a cylinder like a prism?
   _____
   _____

9. How is a cylinder different from a prism?
   _____
   _____

▶ **Nets for Cylinders**

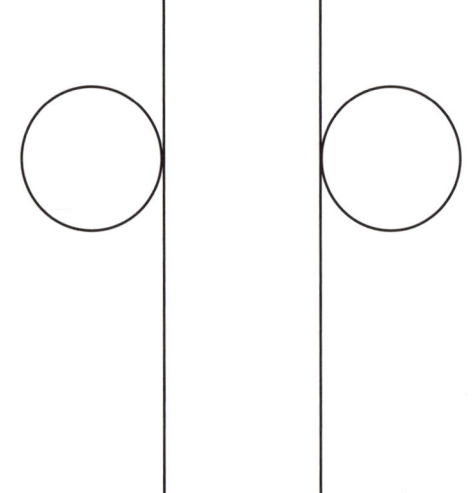

10. Explain how to make a cylinder from this **net**.
    _____
    _____

11. How is the length of the rectangle related to the **circumference** of each circle?
    _____
    _____

372 UNIT E LESSON 1   CA Standards: MG 2.0   Prisms and Cylinders

E–1

Name _____ **Date** _____

Class Activity

▶ **Match Nets and Solids**

Match each net in the first column to a solid in the second column. The nets are smaller than the solids.

12. _____ 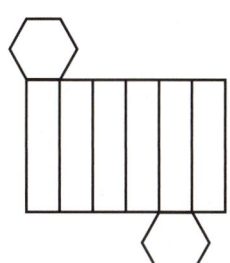   A.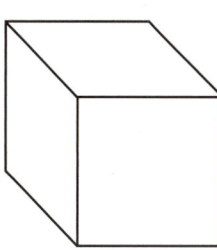

13. _____ 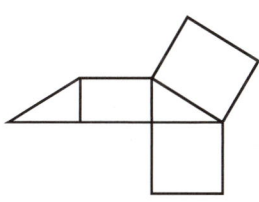   B.

14. _____ 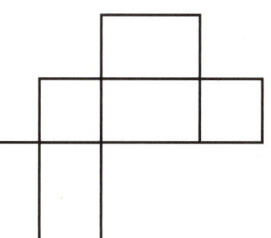   C.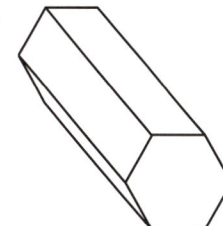

15. _____ 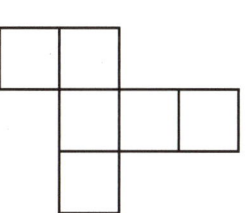   D.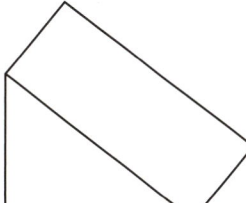

16. _____ 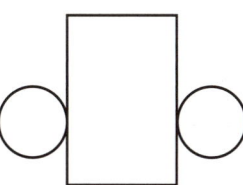   E.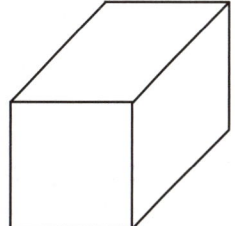

UNIT E LESSON 1   CA Standards: MG 2.0   Prisms and Cylinders 373

▶ Find Surface Area

Vocabulary
surface area

These nets form prisms. Fill in the missing dimensions. Then find the surface area of each prism.

17.

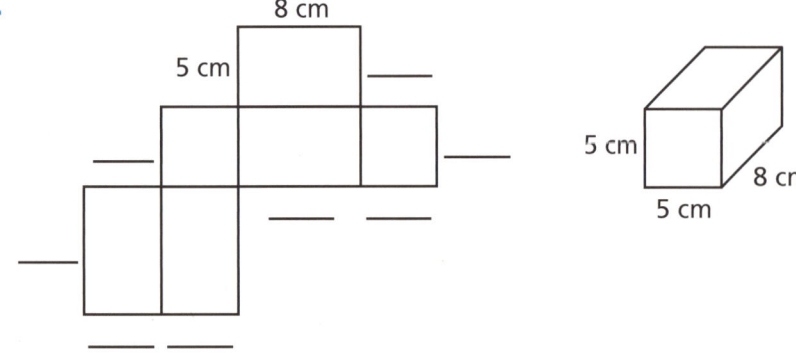

Area of a square base: _____

Area of a rectangle: _____

Surface area: _____

18.

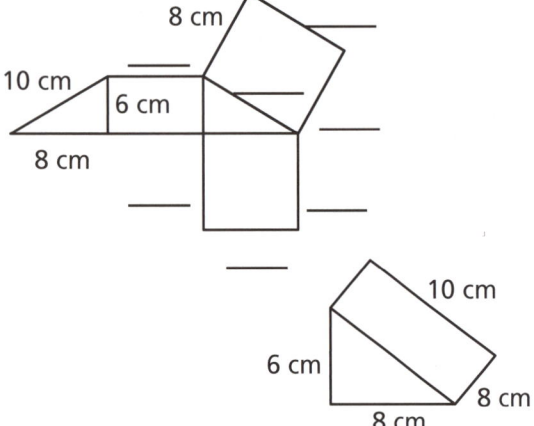

Area of a triangular base: _____

Areas of the rectangles: _____ _____ _____

Surface area: _____

19. How can you find the surface area of any prism?

_____

_____

374 UNIT E LESSON 1   CA Standards: MG 1.0; KEY MG 1.2; MR 2.3   Prisms and Cylinders

Name each prism and find its surface area.

20.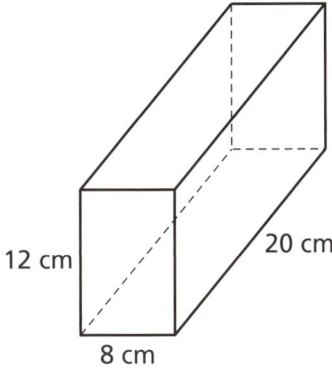

Show your work.

_____

_____

21.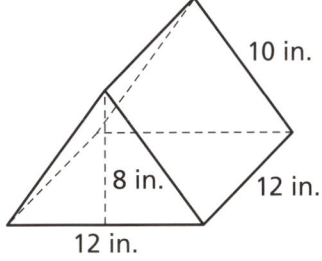

_____

_____

The edges of this cube are 3 cm long.

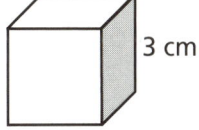

22. What is the area of each **face**?

_____

23. What is the surface area of the cube?

_____

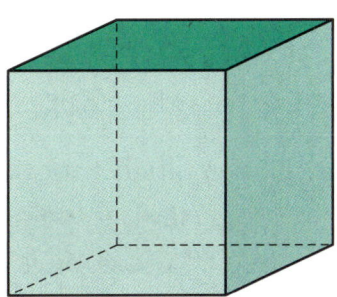

24. Write one sentence that describes how to find the surface area of a cube.

_____

_____

Class Activity   E–1

▶ Solve Problems

A cube has a surface area of 24 square meters.

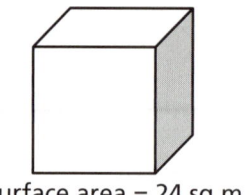
Surface area = 24 sq m

25. What is the area of each face? _____

26. What is the length of each edge? _____

The surface area of a cube is 54 square centimeters.

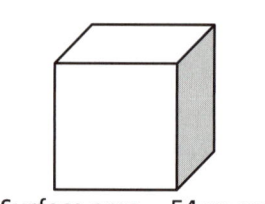
Surface area = 54 sq cm

27. What is the area of each face of the cube?

   _____

28. What is the length of each edge?

   _____

One face of a cube has an area of 16 square millimeters.

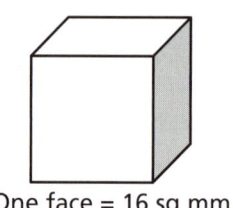
One face = 16 sq mm

29. What is the surface area of the cube?

   _____

30. What is the length of each edge?

   _____

31. What is the volume of the cube?

   _____

A cube has a volume of 8 cubic decimeters.

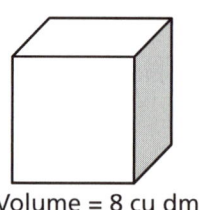
Volume = 8 cu dm

32. What is the length of each edge?

   _____

33. What is the area of each face?

   _____

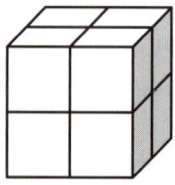

34. Pedro glued together 8 one-inch cubes to make a bigger cube. He then painted the cube red. In square inches, what area of the cube is covered by red paint?

   _____

376 UNIT E LESSON 1   CA Standards: MG 1.0; KEY MG 1.2; KEY MG 1.3   Prisms and Cylinders

Dear Family,

In this unit of *Math Expressions*, your child is studying three-dimensional or solid figures. These figures include prisms, cylinders, pyramids, and cones, as shown below.

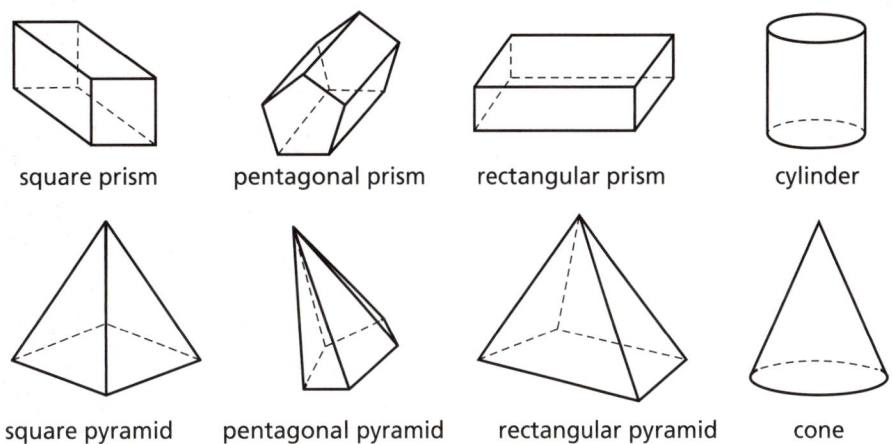

You can become an active part of your child's learning by asking questions about these figures. For example, you might point to a figure and ask:

- What is the name of this figure?
- What is the shape of its base?
- How many bases does it have?
- How many sides does it have?
- What is the shape of each side?

The next unit involves ratios, proportions, and percents. Your child will be required to add, subtract, multiply, and divide. If necessary, encourage your child to practice these operations. If you need practice materials or if you have any questions, please call or write to me.

Sincerely,
Your child's teacher

Estimada familia:

En esta unidad de *Math Expressions*, su niño está estudiando cuerpos geométricos o figuras tridimensionales. Estas figuras incluyen prismas, cilindros, pirámides y conos, como se muestra a continuación.

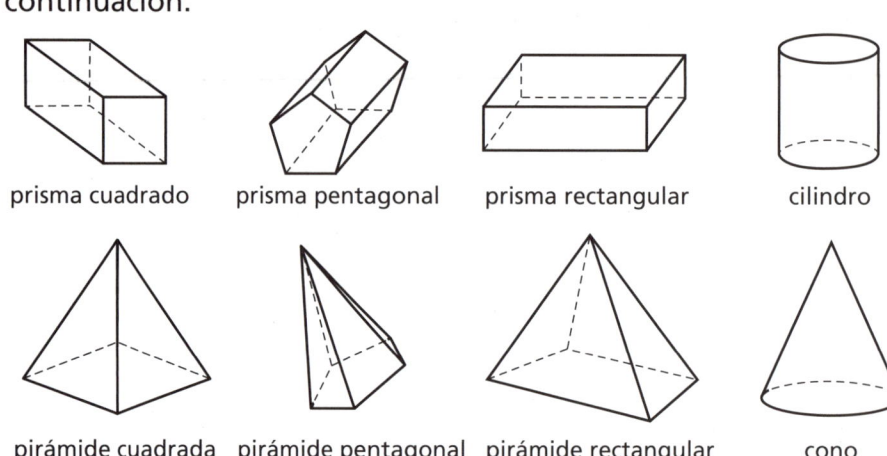

Usted puede participar en el aprendizaje de su niño haciéndole preguntas sobre estas figuras. Por ejemplo, podría señalar una figura y preguntarle:

- ¿Cómo se llama esta figura?
- ¿Cuál es la forma de su base?
- ¿Cuántas bases tiene?
- ¿Cuántos lados tiene?
- ¿Cuál es la forma de cada lado?

La siguiente unidad trata razones, proporciones y porcentajes. A su niño se le pedirá que sume, reste, multiplique y divida. Si es necesario, anime a su niño a practicar estas operaciones. Si necesita materiales para practicar, o si tiene alguna pregunta, por favor comuníquese conmigo.

Atentamente,
El maestro de su niño

E-2 Class Activity

Name _____ Date _____

Vocabulary
cone
apex

▶ **Make a Cone**

A **cone** is a geometric solid with a circular base. When a cone sits on its base, it has a single vertex at the top, called an **apex**.

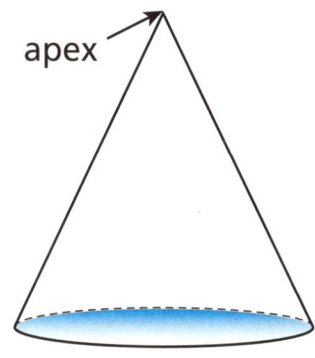
apex

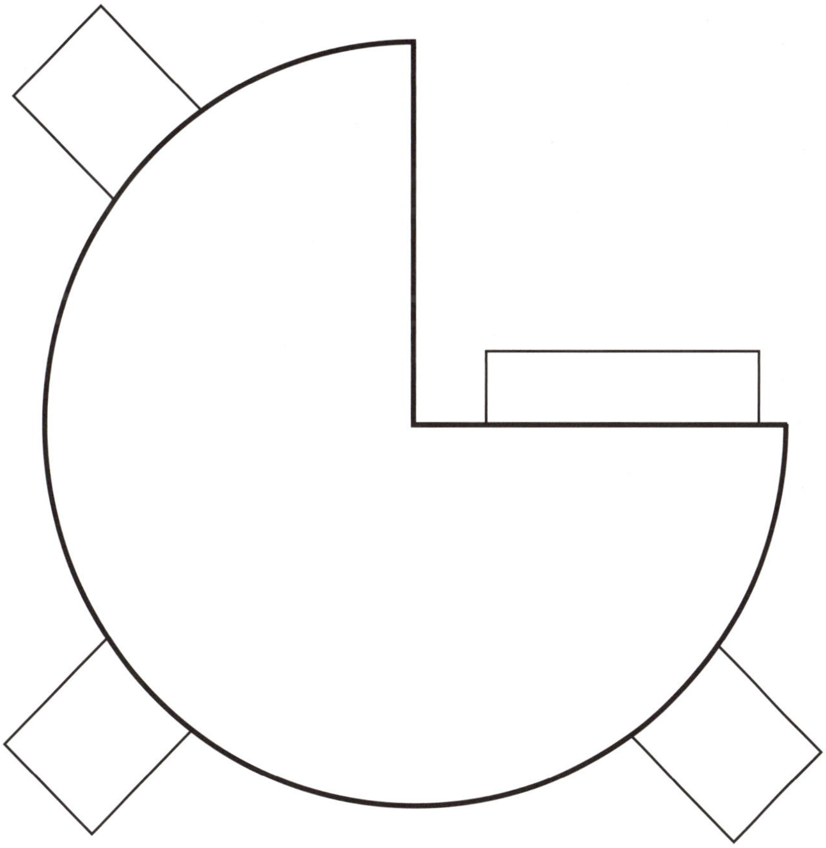

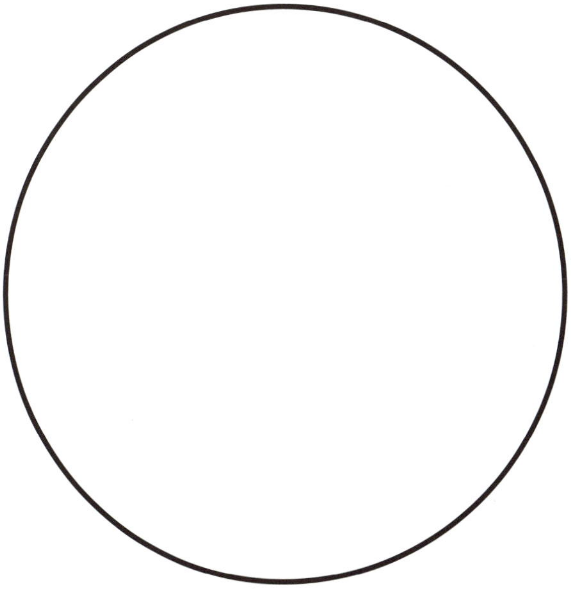

UNIT E LESSON 2   CA Standards: MG 2.0

E–2 Class Activity

▶ Compare Pyramids

Pyramids have been used in architecture for many centuries.

About 4,000 years ago, Egyptians built huge pyramids of stone blocks. These illustrations show two of the three famous pyramids of Giza. They still stand along the Nile River near the city of Cairo.

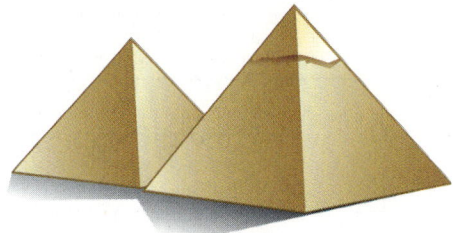

About 2,000 years ago, the Mayan people built step pyramids to help them track the seasons of the year. This illustration shows the step pyramid in Chichen Itza, Mexico.

In 1983, Chinese American architect I.M. Pei was invited to design a glass pyramid for the famous Louvre Museum in Paris, France. This pyramid serves as a skylight for the main entrance to the museum, which is one floor below the pyramid.

A pyramid, like a prism, can have any polygon for a base.

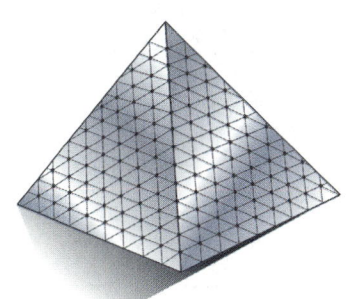

Vocabulary

pyramid

1. What makes pyramids A and B like each other?

   _____

   _____

2. What makes them different?

   _____

3. Write a different name for each pyramid.

   A _____

   B _____

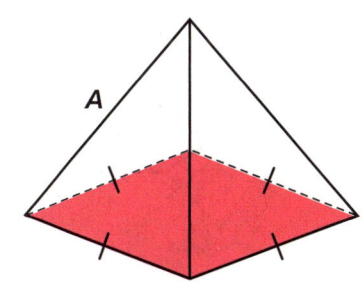

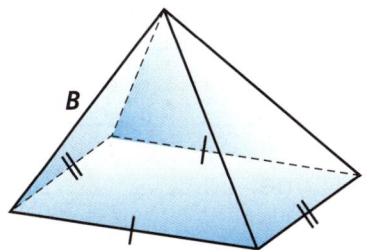

UNIT E LESSON 2   CA Standards: MG 2.0   Pyramids and Cones **381**

4. How is a cone similar to a pyramid?

_____

_____

5. How is a cone different from a pyramid?

_____

_____

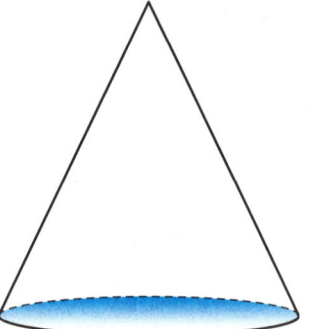

▶ Discuss Pyramids

Name the shape of the base and use it to name the pyramid.

6.

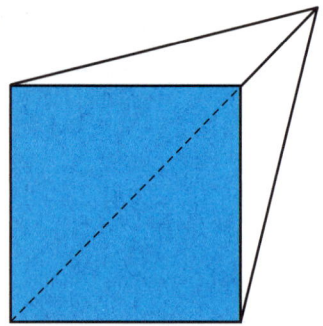

Base: _____

Name: _____
_____

7.

Base: _____

Name: _____
_____

8.

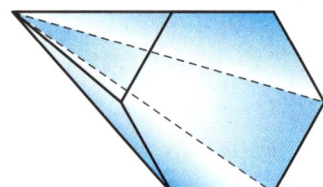

Base: _____

Name: _____
_____

9.

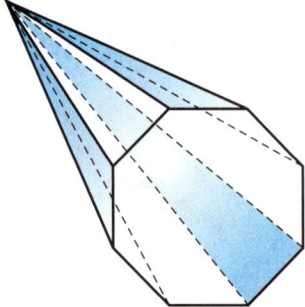

Base: _____

Name: _____
_____

10.

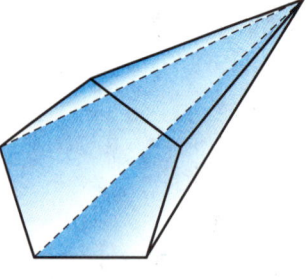

Base: _____

Name: _____
_____

11.

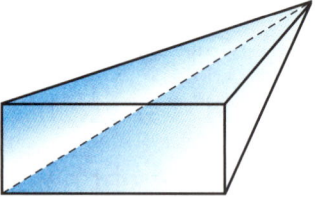

Base: _____

Name: _____
_____

▶ Pyramids and Nets

Match each net to a solid. The nets do not match the solids exactly.

12. _____    A.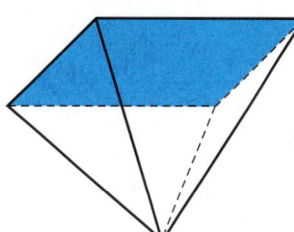

13. _____ 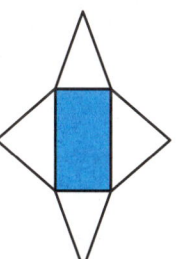   B.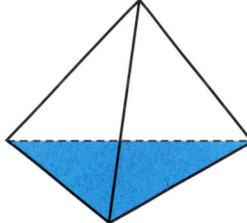

14. _____    C.

15. _____ 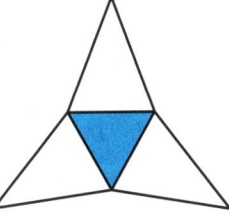   D.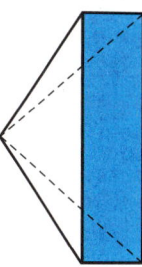

16. _____ 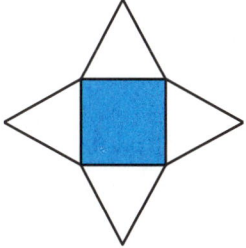   E.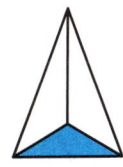

Class Activity

▶ Find Surface Area

These nets form pyramids. Find the surface area of each net.

17.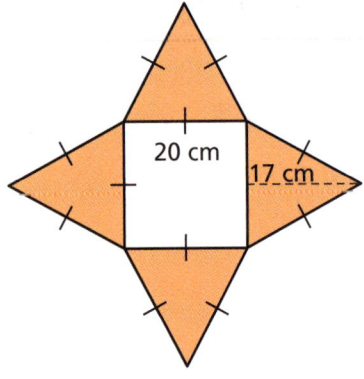

_____

18.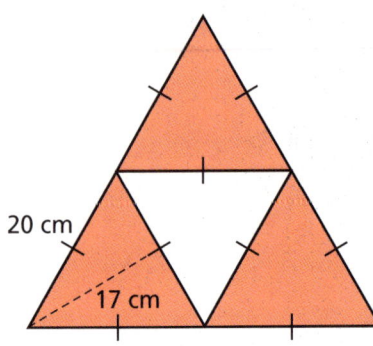

_____

19.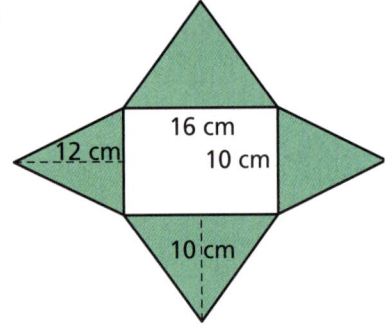

_____

20.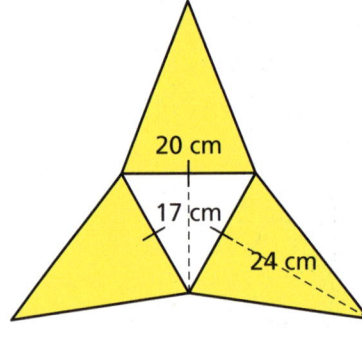

_____

Find the surface area of each pyramid.

21.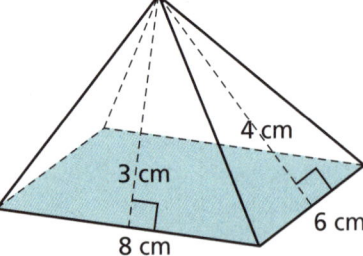

_____

22.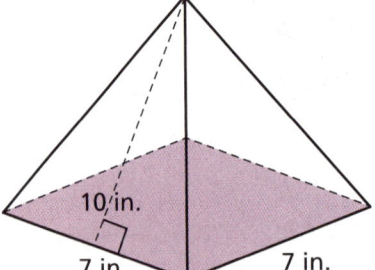

_____

Vocabulary
view

▶ Draw Two-Dimensional Views

These **views** show what a solid figure looks like from the front, side, and top.

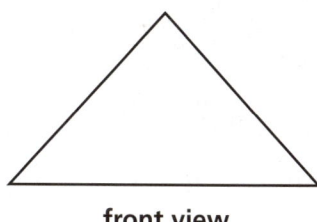

front view   side view   top view

1. Circle the solid that matches the views shown above.

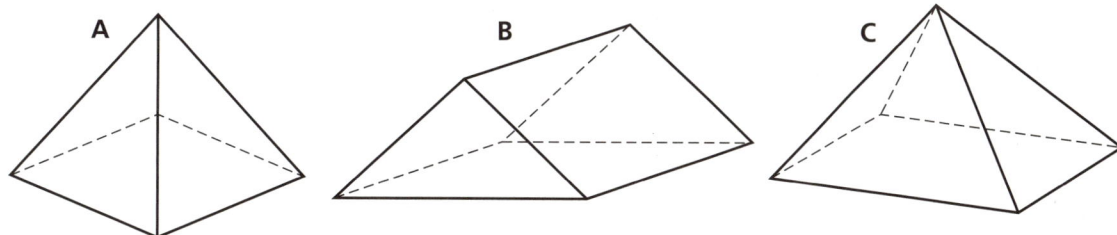

A   B   C

Draw the front, side, and top views of the other two solids. Then name each solid.

2.

front view	side view	top view

Name of Solid: _____

3.

Name of Solid: _____

UNIT E LESSON 3   CA Standards: MG 2.3   Compare and Contrast Geometric Solids **385**

Class Activity E-3

Name _____ Date _____

▶ Draw Pictures of Solids

Below are three different views of the figure at the right.

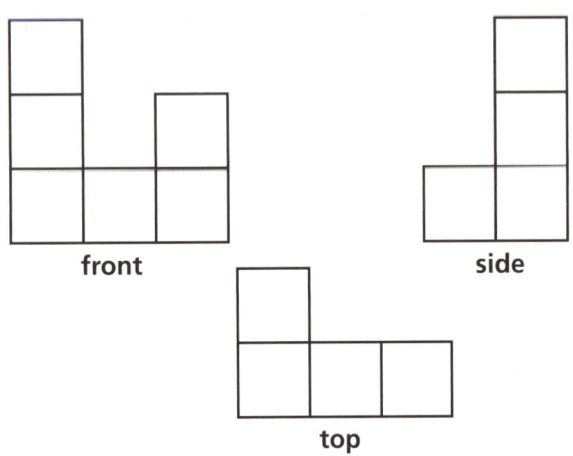

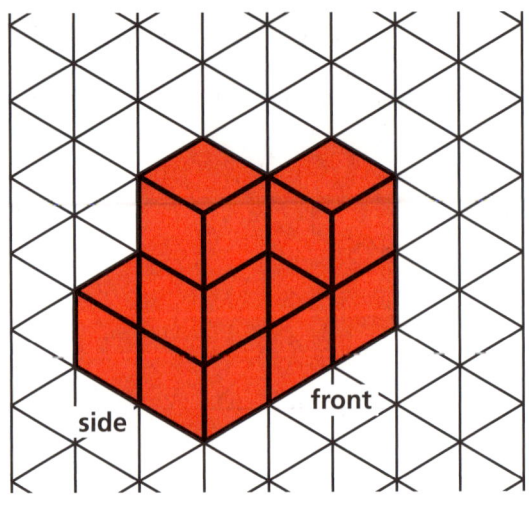

Draw a picture to match the views.

4.
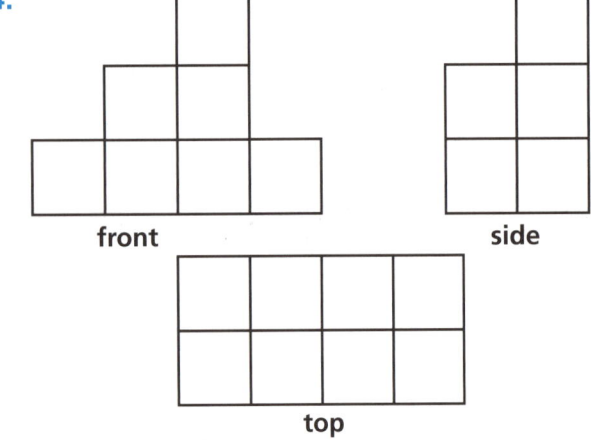

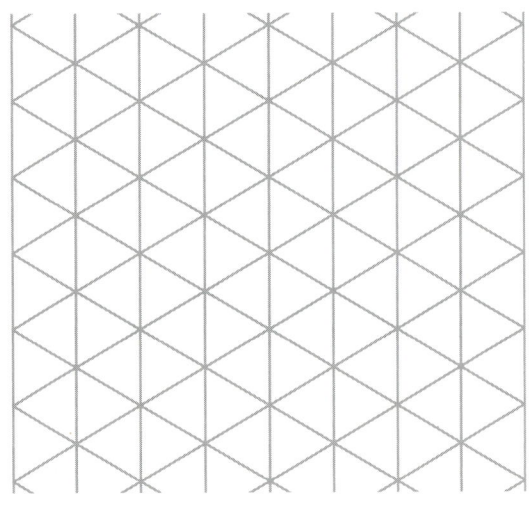

5.
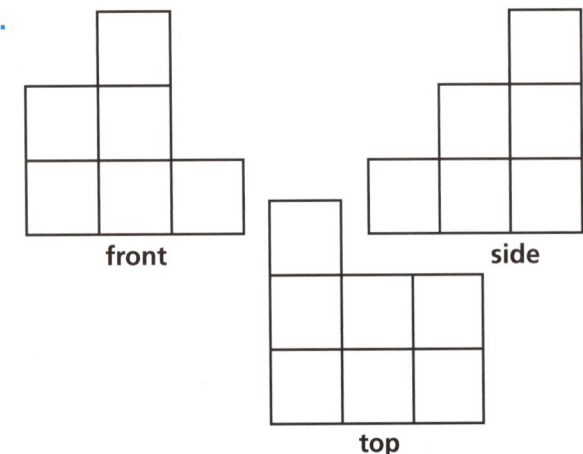

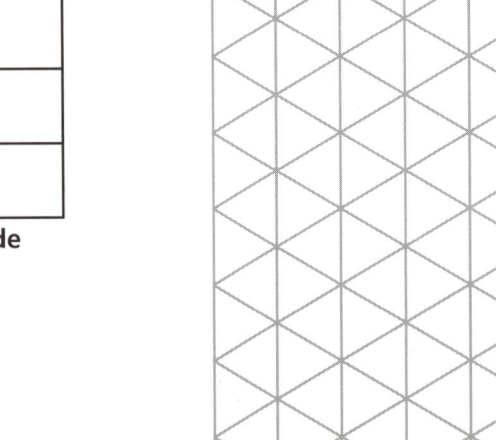

386 UNIT E LESSON 3   CA Standards: MG 2.3   Compare and Contrast Geometric Solids

Name _____ Date _____

Name the solid.

1.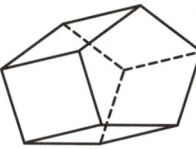

   _____

2.

   _____

3.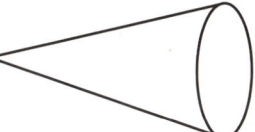

   _____

4.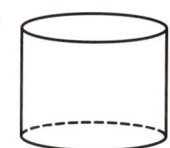

   _____

Find the surface area of each three-dimensional figure.   Show your work.

5.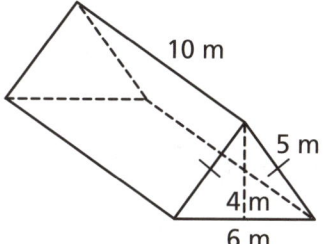

   surface area = _____

6.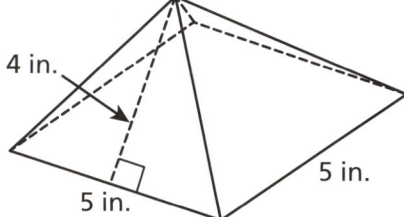

   surface area = _____

UNIT E TEST

387

 Name _____ Date _____

Unit Test

Name the solid that the net makes.

7.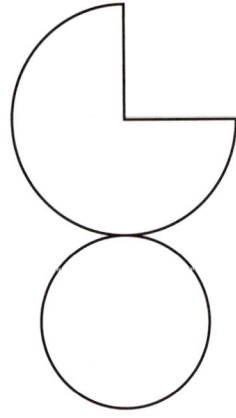

_____

8.

_____

9. Which figure shows the top view of the stack of cubes?

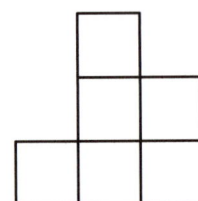 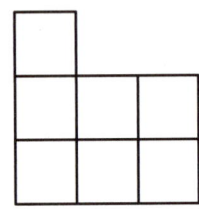 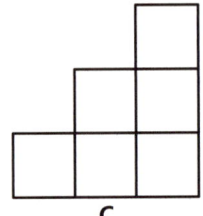 

A B C

10. Name the figure. Draw the views of the figure.

_____

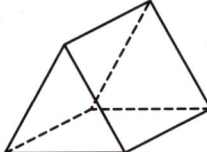

Front	Side	Top

388 UNIT E TEST

6-1 Class Activity

▶ Find the Total So Far

Noreen started to save money. Every day she put three $1 coins into her duck bank. Write how much money she had each day.

On Day 0 Noreen did not put money into her duck bank.		On Day 0 Noreen's duck bank was empty. She had $0.
1. On Day 1 Noreen put $3 into her bank.		On Day 1 Noreen had $_____ in her bank.
2. On Day 2 Noreen put $3 into her bank.		On Day 2 Noreen had $_____ in her bank.
3. On Day 3 Noreen put $3 into her bank.		On Day 3 Noreen had $_____ in her bank.
4. On Day 4 Noreen put $3 into her bank.		On Day 4 Noreen had $_____ in her bank.
5. On Day 5 Noreen put $3 into her bank.		On Day 5 Noreen had $_____ in her bank.
6. On Day 6 Noreen put $3 into her bank.		On Day 6 Noreen had $_____ in her bank.

7. **On the Back** Draw and write how much money Noreen would have in her bank on Day 7 and on Day 8.

UNIT 6 LESSON 1 — Multiplication Patterns

6-1 Class Activity

Name _____ Date _____

Vocabulary
Multiplication Column Table

▶ Complete a Multiplication Column Table

This **Multiplication Column Table** shows Noreen's savings.

8. Fill in the rest of the table to show how much money Noreen saved each day and how much her total was each day.

Days	Dollars
0	0
1	3 +3
2	___
3	___
	___
	___
	___
	___
	___

9. What did you write beside each column?
_____

10. What does the number beside each column show?
_____
_____

▶ Identify Multiplication Column Tables

These tables show four different ways Noreen could have saved money. Complete each table. Then decide which tables are Multiplication Column Tables and which are not. Explain why.

11.
Days	Dollars	
0	0	
1	2	+2
2		+2
3		+2
4		+2
5		+2
6		+2

_____
_____
_____
_____
_____

Name _______________ Date _______________

12.

Days	Dollars
0	0
1	4
2	12
3	18
4	20
5	24
6	28

+4

13.

Days	Dollars
0	0
1	7
2	14
3	21
4	28
5	35
6	42

14.

Days	Dollars
0	0
1	3
2	5
3	5
4	9
5	11
6	14

Dear Family,

In our math class, we are exploring the ideas of ratio and proportion.

The ratio of one number to another is a simple way to express the relative size of two quantities or measurements. For example, the ratio of the lengths of the sides of this rectangle is 3 to 2.

A proportion is an equation that shows two equivalent ratios. It can be written 14 : 6 = 35 : 15   or   14 : 6 : : 35 : 15.

Here is a proportion problem:
Grandfather bought 14 apples for $6. If I buy the same kind of apples, how much will 35 apples cost?

The problem makes this proportion:

14 : 6 = 35 : c

To solve it, we can put the ratios in a Factor Puzzle like your child has been solving all year.

c is 3 × 5 = 15

The Factor Puzzle is from the rows of the ratio table that are ×2 and ×5 of the basic ratio 7 : 3. Factor Puzzles enable your child to understand and solve challenging proportion problems.

Discuss with your child any proportions you use in your life, such as doubling a recipe.

If you have any questions, please call or write to me.

Sincerely,
Your child's teacher

UNIT 6 LESSON 1   Multiplication Patterns **393**

Estimada familia:

En la clase de matemáticas estamos explorando las razones y las proporciones.

La razón de un número a otro es una manera simple de expresar el tamaño relativo de dos cantidades o medidas. Por ejemplo, la razón de las longitudes de los lados de este rectángulo es de 3 a 2.

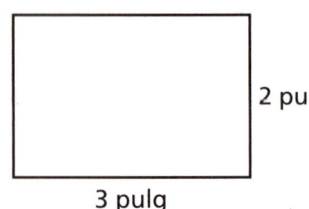

Una proporción es una ecuación que muestra 2 razones equivalentes. Se puede escribir 14 : 6 = 35 : 15   ó   14 : 6 : : 35 : 15

Éste es un problema de proporción:
El abuelo compró 14 manzanas con $6.
Si compro el mismo tipo de manzanas,
¿cuánto costarán 35 manzanas?

El problema hace esta proporción:

$$14 : 6 = 35 : c$$

Para resolverlo, podemos poner las razones en un rompecabezas de factores como los que su niño ha resuelto durante el año.

$$c \text{ es } 3 \times 5 = 15$$

El rompecabezas de factores se forma con las filas de la tabla que son × 2 y × 5 de la razón básica 7 : 3. Los rompecabezas de factores ayudan a su niño a comprender y resolver problemas complicados de proporciones.

Comente con su niño sólo las proporciones que usan en la vida diaria, tales como duplicar una receta de cocina.

Si tiene preguntas, por favor comuníquese conmigo.

Atentamente,
El maestro de su niño

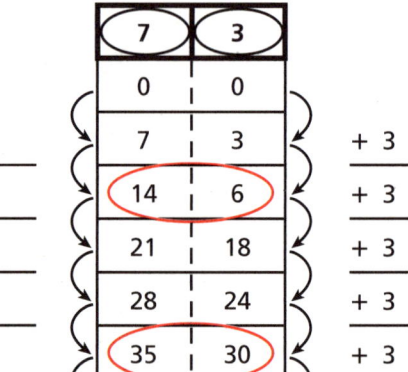

6-2 Class Activity

Vocabulary
unit

▶ Use Unit Rate Language

Write each phrase in your own words. Do not use *per*.

1. 7 days per week _____

2. 9 feet *per* second _____

3. 9 books *per* shelf _____

4. $7 *per* sack of rice _____

▶ Use Different Units and Groups

Every Multiplication Column Situation is divided into **units**, and describes a constant group for each unit. Which of these are Multiplication Column Situations? For each one:

• tell the unit and group per unit

• write the situation using the word *per*.

5. In the zoo, 7 kangaroos live in each of the kangaroo living areas.

_____
_____

6. The band marched on the field one row at a time. There were six people in every row.

_____
_____

7. Pedro and Pilar collect snails. Each day they add 4 snails to their terrarium.

_____
_____

8. Last week Ben saw 3 films, this week he saw 4 films, and next week he will see 2 films.

_____

6-2 Class Activity

9. A hot-air balloon is rising up from the school baseball field. It rises 9 feet every second.

   _____

   _____

10. A bagging machine was set to place the same number of oranges in each bag. Today none of the settings stay fixed. The machine places 3 and then 5 and then 9 oranges in bags.

    _____

11. Every day this week Joanne made 3 of her 7 free throws during basketball practice.

    _____

    _____

12. Sandy loves crossword puzzles. She can solve 8 clues each minute.

    _____

    _____

13. Farmer Brown is driving his tractor down his hilly and flat fields. He can plough 7 rows per hour on the flat field. On the hilly field he sometimes ploughs 6 and sometimes only 5 rows each hour.

    _____

Make a Multiplication Column Table for the situations in exercises 5 and 6.

14.

Unit	Rate
Living Area	Kangaroos
0	
		+___
		+___
		+___
		+___
		+___
		+___

15.

Unit	Rate
Rows	People
0	
		+___
		+___
		+___
		+___
		+___
		+___
		+___

396 UNIT 6 LESSON 2   Unit Rate

▶ Describe a Multiplication Column Situation

Decide if each situation is a Multiplication Column Situation. Write the unit and group for stories that are Multiplication Column Situations. Write "no" if it is not a Multiplication Column Situation.

1. Each fish tank has 4 snails to help keep the tanks clean.

   Unit: _____

   Group (the unit rate): _____

2. Everyone in the Green family had 2 eggs for breakfast yesterday

   Unit: _____

   Group (the unit rate): _____

3. Tara makes 9 drawings on each page of her sketchbook.

   Unit: _____

   Group: _____

4. Erin puts 3 large photos on 1 shelf and 7 small photos on 1 shelf.

   Unit: _____

   Group: _____

5. Jonathan saves $8 every week, but last week he spent some of his savings to go to a movie.

   Unit: _____

   Group: _____

6. Fred planted 7 tomato vines in each yard he takes care of.

   Unit: _____

   Group: _____

7. Mr. Gomez used 3 boxes of markers in his classroom last week. This week he used 2 boxes of markers.

   Unit: _____

   Group: _____

6-3 Class Activity

Name _____ Date _____

8. Abby uses 2 cups of flour in each loaf of bread she makes.

   Unit: _____

   Group: _____

9. Laurie saved the same amount of money each week. After 10 weeks she had $80.

   Unit: _____

   Group: _____

▶ Write a Definition

10. Write a definition of Multiplication Column Situation and discuss your definition.

    _____

    _____

    _____

▶ Identify Multiplication Column Tables

Decide whether each table is a Multiplication Column Table. Explain why or why not.

11. _____ _____

0	0
1	9
2	18
3	27
4	36
5	45

12. _____ _____

0	0
1	4
2	5
3	9
4	10
5	14

13. _____ _____

0	0
1	11
2	22
3	33
4	44
5	55

14. _____ _____

0	0
1	3
2	5
3	8
4	10
5	13

_____ _____ _____ _____

_____ _____ _____ _____

15. Write in your Math Journal or tell a different story for each table. Then label each table.

6-4 Class Activity

▶ Linked Multiplication Column Table Situations

Vocabulary
Linked Multiplication Column Table
Ratio Table

Noreen saves $3 a day. Tim saves $5 a day. They start saving on the same day. The **Linked Multiplication Column Table** and the **Ratio Table** show Noreen's and Tim's savings.

Linked Multiplication Column Table

Days	Noreen ③	Tim ⑤
0	0	0
1	3	5
2	6	10
3	9	15
4	12	20
5	15	25
6	18	30
7	21	35

Ratio Table

N	T
3	5
0	0
3	5
6	10
9	15
12	20
15	25
18	30
21	35

1. How are the tables alike? How are they different?

   _____
   _____
   _____
   _____

2. Fill in the numbers at each side of the Ratio Table to show Noreen's and Tim's constant increases.

Use the tables to answer each question.

3. Noreen has saved $12. How much has Tim saved? On which day is this?

   _____

4. Tim has saved $35. How much has Noreen saved? On which day is this?

   _____

5. On what day will Noreen have $30 in her duck bank? How much will Tim have then?

UNIT 6 LESSON 4 — Linked Stories Are Ratios **399**

6-4 Class Activity

▶ Create a Ratio Table

Noreen and Tim bought lots of bags of oranges. Each of Tim's bags cost $6, but Noreen paid only $2 for each bag on sale.

6. Complete the tables for Noreen and Tim. The linking unit is bags of oranges.

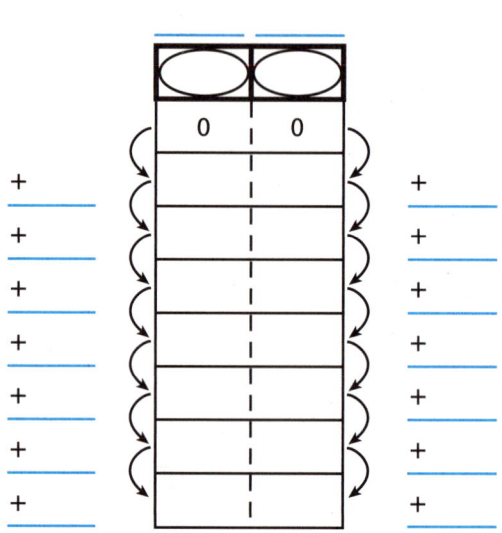

Ratio Table

7. How much did 2 bags of oranges cost Noreen? _____ Tim? _____ How much did 4 bags of oranges cost Noreen? _____ Tim? _____

Noreen and Tim plant carrots in their garden. Noreen plants 4 carrot seeds in each row. Tim plants 9 carrot seeds in each row.

8. Fill in the table about Noreen and Tim. The linking unit is _____.

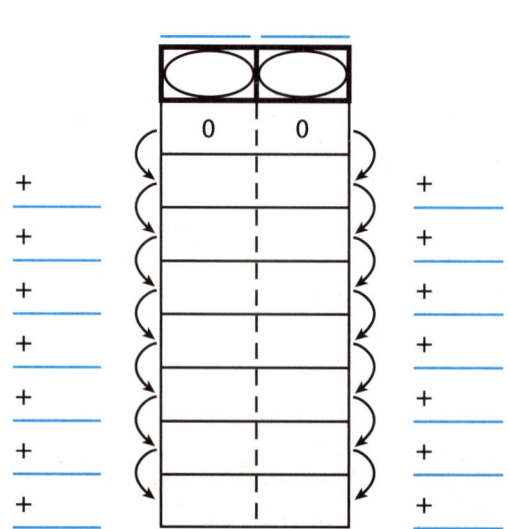

Ratio Table

400 UNIT 6 LESSON 4 — Linked Stories Are Ratios

6-4 Class Activity

9. How many carrot seeds will Noreen and Tim each have planted after they have planted 3 rows? _____
   6 rows? _____
   7 rows? _____

Noreen makes 5 drawings on each page of her sketchbook. Tim makes smaller drawings, so he has 7 drawings on each page of his sketchbook.

10. Fill in the tables. The linking unit is _____.

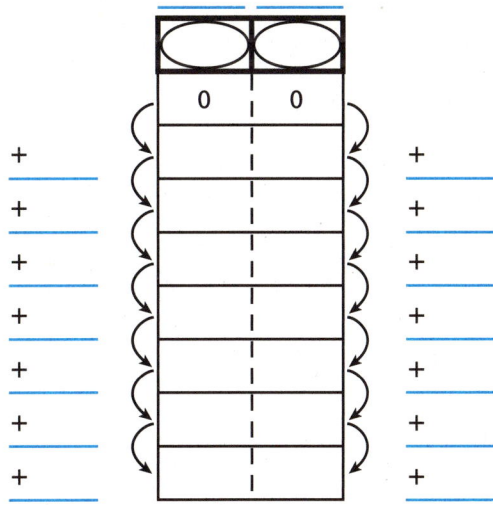

Linked Multiplication Column Table   **Ratio Table**

11. What do your tables show about Noreen's and Tim's sketchbooks?

    _____

    _____

    How many drawings do Noreen and Tim each have after they have filled 3 pages? _____
    How many would each have after 5 pages?

    _____

    How many would each have after 10 pages?

    _____

    How many would each have after 101 pages?

    _____

UNIT 6 LESSON 4   Linked Stories Are Ratios

▶ Recognize Ratio and Non-Ratio Tables

12. Which two tables could be Linked Multiplication Column Tables for Noreen and Tim stories? Why?

_____
_____
_____
_____

A.

0	0	0
1	4	7
2	8	14
3	12	21
4	16	28
5	20	35
6	24	42
7	28	49
8	32	56
9	36	63
10	40	70

B.

0	0	0
1	1	5
2	2	12
3	4	18
4	7	20
5	9	24
6	15	30
7	19	33
8	24	42
9	25	48
10	30	50

C.

0	0	0
1	2	9
2	4	18
3	6	27
4	8	36
5	10	45
6	12	54
7	14	63
8	16	72
9	18	81
10	20	90

D.

0	0	0
1	2	3
2	5	6
3	7	9
4	11	12
5	13	15
6	16	18
7	20	21
8	22	24
9	23	27
10	28	30

13. Why are the other tables not Linked Multiplication Column Tables?

_____

14. Tell a Noreen and Tim story for each of the Linked Multiplication Column Tables above.

_____
_____
_____
_____
_____

6-5 Class Activity

Vocabulary
proportion
basic ratio

▶ **Proportions and Factor Puzzles**

A **proportion** problem comes from a ratio situation. It uses two rows from a Ratio Table. Two multiples of a ratio make a proportion.

A proportion is written in the form

or
$$28 : 12 = 70 : 30$$
$$28 : 12 :: 70 : 30$$

This proportion is read as "28 is to 12 as 70 is to 30."

Here is a proportion problem:
Grandfather bought 14 apples for $6. If I buy the same kind of apples, how much will 35 apples cost?

The problem makes this proportion:
$$14 : 6 = 35 : c$$

To solve the proportion and the problem, you need to find the value of c.

1. Fill in the Ratio Table for the problem.

2. Circle the rows of the Ratio Table that make the proportion problem.

    You know how to solve Factor Puzzles. It is faster to make a Factor Puzzle than a whole ratio table.

3. Fill in the Factor Puzzle using the numbers in the rows you circled.

4. What is the solution to the apple proportion?

   _____

   _____

5. You wrote numbers above the Factor Puzzle. Where are they in the ratio table?

   _____

   This top row of the Ratio Table can be called the **basic ratio**. It is from the _____ row of the multiplication table.

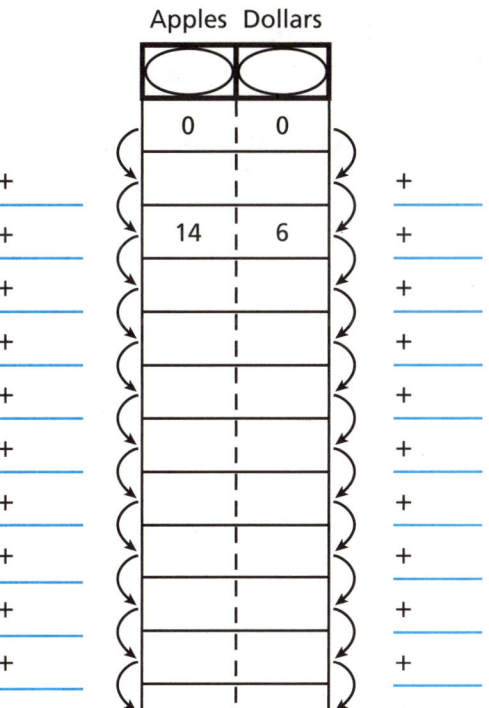

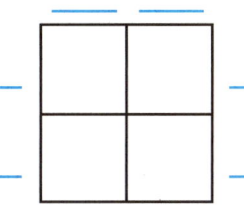

UNIT 6 LESSON 5 — What Are Proportion Situations? **403**

6-5 Class Activity

Name _____ **Date** _____

Vocabulary
Factor Puzzle

▶ **Solve Proportion Problems**

A proportion problem gives you three of the four numbers in a proportion. You can solve a proportion problem by making a Factor Puzzle to show those 2 rows of the Ratio Table.

Use Factor Puzzles to solve these proportion problems about Noreen and Tim.

6. When Noreen planted 6 tomatoes, Tim planted 10 tomatoes. If Noreen plants 21 tomatoes, how many will Tim plant?

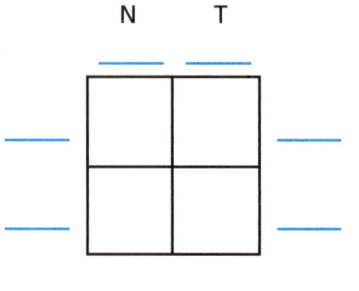

7. When Noreen had 6 stickers, Tim had 21 stickers. How many stickers will Noreen have when Tim has 56?

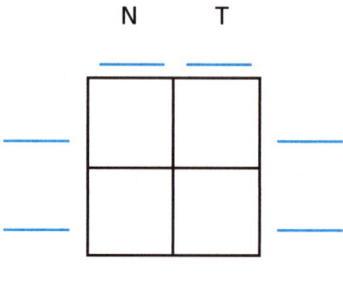

8. Noreen did 72 push-ups while Tim did 32 push-ups. Earlier, while Tim did 12 push-ups, how many did Noreen do? _____

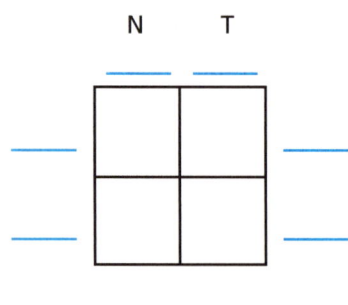

404 UNIT 6 LESSON 5

What Are Proportion Situations?

6–5 Class Activity

▶ Solve on Your Own

Solve these proportion problems about the twins, Diana and Walter. For each problem, make and solve a Factor Puzzle. For problems 9 and 10, use the basic ratio you find beside the Factor Puzzle to make a Ratio Table. Circle the rows of the Ratio Table that make the Factor Puzzle.

9. Diana read 15 pages and Walter read 35. How many pages had Diana read when Walter had read 14?

   _____

10. Diana sold 35 tickets and Walter sold 56. How many tickets had Walter sold when Diana had sold 15?

    _____

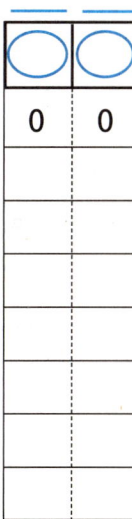

11. Diana sliced 30 bananas while Walter sliced 20. When Diana had sliced 21 bananas, how many had Walter sliced?

    _____

UNIT 6 LESSON 5 — What Are Proportion Situations?

6-5 Class Activity

Name _____ Date _____

▶ **Think About Proportions**

Make Factor Puzzles to solve the proportion problems below. Tell what you assume about each proportion problem. Label each Factor Puzzle. Circle the unknown number in each puzzle and use it to answer the question.

12. Two bands march onto the football field. When Band 1 has 15 people on the field, Band 2 has 6. When Band 2 has 14 people on the field, how many people will Band 1 have?

13. Joshua has 32 angelfish for every 12 snails. When he has 72 angelfish, how many snails will he have?

14. Ann planted 25 rose bushes while Ivan planted 30. How many rose bushes had Ivan planted when Ann had planted 15?

406 UNIT 6 LESSON 5   What Are Proportion Situations?

Solve Problems With Factor Puzzles

Circle the number of each problem that is a proportion problem, and then solve it with a Factor Puzzle. Find the basic ratio in each Factor Puzzle. If a problem is not a proportion problem, tell why.

1. John can plant 7 tomato vines in the time it takes Joanna to plant 4 tomato vines. How many tomato vines will Joanna have planted when John has planted 42 tomato vines?

   _____

   _____

2. Mr. Tally's class uses 2 bags of markers each week. Ms. Petro's class uses 3 bags of markers one week and 2 the next. If Mr. Tally used 14 bags of markers, how many did Ms. Petro use?

   _____

   _____

3. In the summer Jason's pond had 14 minnows for each 6 goldfish. Now it has 27 goldfish. How many minnows does it have now?

   _____

   _____

4. Tom is 12 years old. He is 8 years older than his sister Sylvia. How old were Tom and Sylvia 3 years ago?

   _____

   _____

► Factor Puzzle Multiples in a Ratio Table

Central Middle School has 6 computers and 14 printers. If East Middle School in the same district has 28 printers, how many computers does it have?

Here is the Factor Puzzle for this problem. Use the basic ratio from the top of the Factor Puzzle to fill in the Ratio Table.

```
          C    P
          3    7
     2 |  6  | 14 | 2
     4 | 12  | 28 | 4
          3    7
```

5. How do the numbers 2 and 4, which are at the sides of the Factor Puzzle, relate to the Ratio Table?

_____

6. Where are they in the multiplication table?

_____

Solve the problems below. Make your own Factor Puzzles if you need them.

When there are 6 banana slices in Diana's fruit salad, there are 14 orange pieces.

7. When there are 28 orange pieces in the fruit salad, how many banana slices are there?

_____

8. When there are 56 orange pieces in the fruit salad, how many banana slices are there?

_____

9. When there are 18 banana slices in the fruit salad, how many orange pieces are there?

_____

Show your work.

408 UNIT 6 LESSON 6   Solve Proportion Problems

▶ Solve Numeric Proportion Problems

Solve each proportion by making a Factor Puzzle on another sheet of paper. Then write the basic ratio for each.

1. _____ : 32 = 15 : 40   _____
2. 16 : 36 = _____ : 63   _____
3. 42 : _____ = 54 : 63   _____
4. 14 : 56 = 6 : _____   _____

▶ Identify and Solve Proportion Problems

Tell which are proportion problems. Explain why the others are not. Solve the proportion problems using Factor Puzzles or another method.

5. A bag of 6 oranges costs $2. How many oranges will I get for $10?

6. Cal is 19 and his sister is 13. How old was Cal when his sister was 8?

7. You can make 8 pies from 30 pounds of apples. How many pies can you make from 15 pounds of apples?

8. In the zoo, there are 6 flamingos for every 8 ducks. If there are 20 ducks, how many flamingos are there?

9. Alice is a mail carrier. Today she is delivering letters on Maple Street. She has letters for people living in houses #4 and #6. If she has letters for house #20, what other house do you think she may have letters for?

10. Dana and Sue are sisters. Every week the sisters get an allowance. Dana is older than Sue so she gets more allowance. Now Dana has $48 and Sue has $36. How much will Dana have when Sue has $54?

UNIT 6 LESSON 7   Solve Proportions as Factor Puzzles **409**

6–7 Class Activity

▶ Find the Table That Matches a Problem

Cross out the table that is not a Ratio Table. Circle the rows in each Ratio Table for the proportion. Fill in the basic ratio in the blue circles. Write which story from the previous page is represented by each table. One table does not represent a story.

11. ◯ : ◯

0 : 0
1 : 3
2 : 6
3 : 9
4 : 12
5 : 15
6 : 18
7 : 21

_____

12. ◯ : ◯

0 : 0
6 : 2
12 : 4
18 : 6
24 : 8
30 : 10
36 : 12
42 : 14
48 : 16

_____

13. ◯ : ◯

0 : 0
4 : 3
8 : 6
12 : 9
16 : 12
20 : 15
24 : 18
28 : 21
32 : 24
36 : 27
40 : 30
44 : 33
48 : 36

_____

14. ◯ : ◯

0 : 0
1 : 0
2 : 0
3 : 0
4 : 0
5 : 0
6 : 0
7 : 1
8 : 2
9 : 3
10 : 4
11 : 5
12 : 6
13 : 7
14 : 8
15 : 9
16 : 10
17 : 11
18 : 12
19 : 13
20 : 14

_____

15. On a separate sheet of paper, choose one of your favorite Multiplication Table situations that you wrote on an earlier day and change it to a proportion problem. Make a Ratio Table for your problem.

Use the Basic Ratio

Solve the proportion problems below using Factor Puzzles, and then solve them using a different method.

1. Danny filled each vase with 5 roses and 9 irises. How many irises would he need if he uses 30 roses?

   _____

2. $2 : 7 = 10 : y$

   _____

Solve Problems

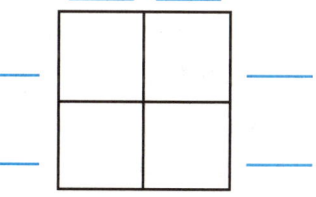

Tell whether each problem is a proportion problem or not. Tell why you think so, explaining the assumptions you made. Then solve the problem.

3. Martha and Beth walk home from school at different rates. When Martha walks 35 feet, Beth walks 15 feet. How far has Martha walked when Beth has walked 30 feet?

   _____

   _____

4. If I have 20 blue marbles and 25 red marbles, what is the ratio of blue to red marbles? How many red marbles would be in the same ratio to 8 blue marbles?

   _____

   _____

   _____

5. Maggie bought vegetables at the farmers' market. She chose 6 tomatoes and 9 broccoli bunches. Then she chose 8 carrots. How many heads of lettuce do you think Maggie chose?

   _____

   _____

6. Every day, Mark and Wanda watch *Nature Journal* together, but Wanda has missed some of the episodes. When Mark had seen 7, Wanda had seen 4. When Mark had seen 10, how many episodes had Wanda seen?

_____

_____

_____

_____

Match three tables with the problems from 3, 4, 5, and 6 that they represent. Which table does not match any problem? Cross out any table that is not a Ratio Table. Circle the rows that make the proportions and fill in the basic ratios in the blue circles.

7.

○	○
0	0
1	0
2	0
3	0
4	1
5	2
6	3
7	4
8	5
9	6
10	7

8.

○	○
0	0
5	3
10	4
15	5
20	6
25	7
30	8
35	9
40	10
45	20
50	22

9.

○	○
0	0
7	3
14	6
21	9
28	12
35	15
42	18
49	21
56	24
63	27
70	30

10.

○	○
0	0
4	5
8	10
12	15
16	20
20	25
24	30
28	35
32	40
36	45
40	50

_____

_____

_____

_____

6–9 Class Activity

Name _______________ Date _______________

▶ Write Proportion Problems

Make up a proportion problem for each proportion. Then solve the problem.

1. 24 : 36 = 14 : ______

2. ______ : 24 = 56 : 32

Practice Solving Proportion Problems

Decide whether each problem is a proportion problem. Then solve the problem.

Show your work.

3. A turtle crawled 21 meters in 12 minutes. How long did it take her to crawl 14 meters if she crawled at the same rate the whole time?

4. At the Party Store 3 big balloons cost $2. How much will 24 big balloons cost?

5. Every month the public library purchases 10 new fiction books and 7 new DVDs. When the library has purchased 56 new DVDs, how many fiction books will it have purchased?

6. John and Bill drove to Utah for their vacation. They both drove their cars at the same pace, but they left on different days. John left on Day 1 and Bill left 3 days later on Day 4. John got to Utah on Day 6. What day did Bill get to Utah?

7. Mr. Munchkin owns a donut bakery downtown. His donut-making machine is pretty good. Out of every 9 donuts, only 2 are not absolutely perfect. He sells these donuts for less. One day, he baked 54 donuts. How many were not perfect?

8. Two trucks left the dock at exactly the same time and traveled at steady rates. When the first truck had traveled 15 miles, the second truck had traveled 45 miles. How far will the second truck have traveled when the first truck has traveled 30 miles?

6–10 Class Activity

Vocabulary
percent

▶ **Introduce Percent**

1. Circle each **percent** of the 100 pennies.

   1%   5%   10%   14%

   20%   37%   50%   62%

   75%   89%   100%.

$1.00 = 100 pennies

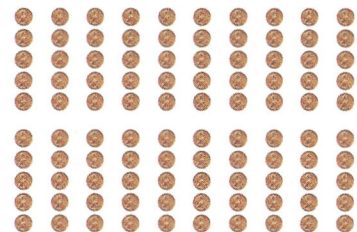

2. Use the percents in exercise 1. Mark each percent on the 100-millimeter line.

   | 1 decimeter = 10 centimeters |
   | = 100 millimeters |

3. Use the percents in exercise 1. Label the last square centimeter that represents each percent of the 100 square centimeters.

| 1 square decimeter |
| = 100 square centimeters |

UNIT 6 LESSON 10   CA Standards: KEY NS 1.2   The Meaning of Percent **415**

Class Activity

▶ **Relate Percents, Fractions, and Decimals**

For each exercise, show each percent of the dollar, decimeter, and square decimeter. Fill in the unknown numbers.

4. $10\% = \dfrac{10}{100} = \dfrac{}{10}$
   $= 0.10 = 0.1$

5. $20\% = \dfrac{}{100} = \dfrac{}{10} = \dfrac{}{5}$
   $= \underline{} = \underline{}$

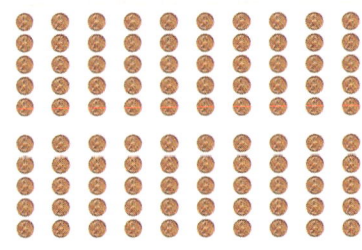

6. $30\% = \dfrac{}{100} = \dfrac{}{10}$
   $= \underline{} = \underline{}$

7. $40\% = \dfrac{}{100} = \dfrac{}{10} = \dfrac{}{5}$
   $= \underline{} = \underline{}$

8. $50\% = \dfrac{}{100} = \dfrac{}{10} = \dfrac{}{2}$
   $= \underline{} = \underline{}$

9. $60\% = \dfrac{}{100} = \dfrac{}{10} = \dfrac{}{5}$
   $= \underline{} = \underline{}$

10. $70\% = \dfrac{}{100} = \dfrac{}{10}$
    $= \underline{} = \underline{}$

11. $80\% = \dfrac{}{100} = \dfrac{}{10} = \dfrac{}{5}$
    $= \underline{} = \underline{}$

12. $90\% = \dfrac{}{100} = \dfrac{}{10}$
    $= \underline{} = \underline{}$

13. $100\% = \dfrac{}{100} = \dfrac{}{10} = \dfrac{}{5} = \dfrac{}{1}$
    $= \underline{}$

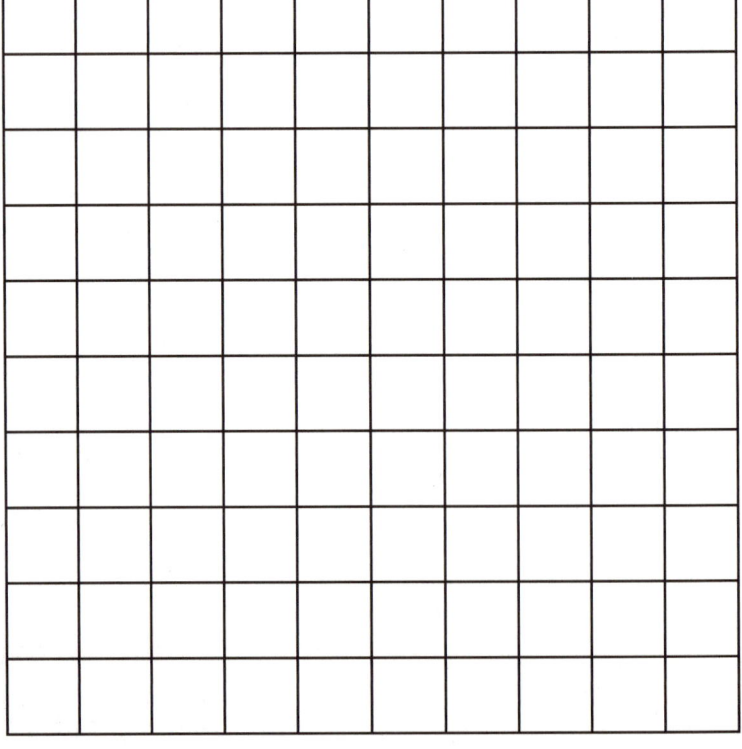

416 UNIT 6 LESSON 10 CA Standards: KEY NS 1.2; MR 2.3 The Meaning of Percent

Name _____ Date _____

14. Use a ruler to draw lines across the page from each percent to connect the equivalent fractions.

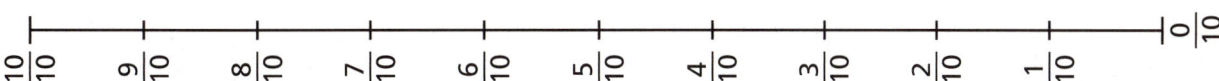
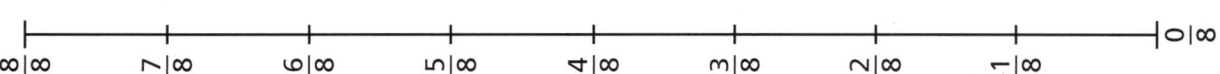
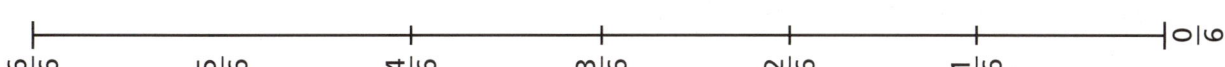

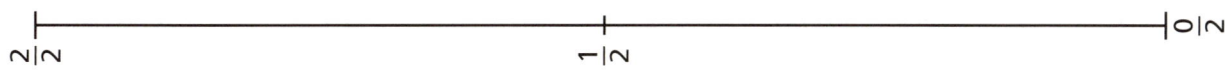
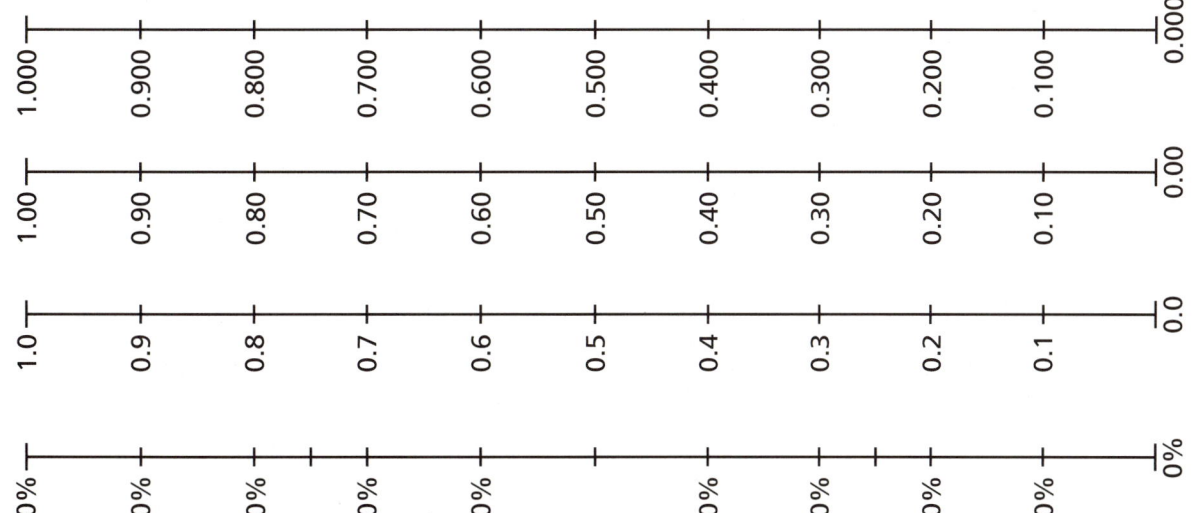

Practice Percent Equivalencies

15. Fill in the missing percents, decimals, and fractions.

		Percent, Decimal, and Fraction Equivalencies			
Cents	Percent of a dollar	Dollars	Decimal	Fraction of 100	Simplest fraction
40 ¢	40%	$0.40	0.40	$\frac{40}{100}$	$\frac{2}{5}$
75 ¢					
	25%				
			0.50		
			0.60		
				$\frac{30}{100}$	
					$\frac{4}{5}$
		$1.00			
		$0.10			
					$\frac{9}{10}$
				$\frac{20}{100}$	
	70%				

Name _____ Date _____

▶ **Solve Percent Problems With Diagrams**

Solve the problems. Use what you know about fractions and percents.

This is 20% of a figure.

☐

1. Draw 80% of the figure.

2. Draw 100% of the figure.

3. Draw 120% of the figure.

4. Draw 200% of the figure.

This is 25% of a figure. ☐

5. Draw 100% of the figure.

6. Draw 150% of the figure.

UNIT 6 LESSON 11  Solve Problems Using Percents **419**

This is 75% of a figure.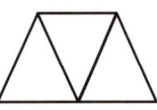

7. Draw 100% of the figure.

8. Draw 25% of the figure.

Here is 75% of a design.

9. Draw 100% of the design.

10. Draw 150% of the design.

11. This is 150% of a figure.

Draw 100% of the figure.

This is 200% of a square.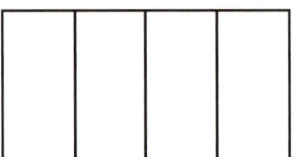

12. Draw the square.

13. Draw 150% of the square.

6-11 Class Activity

▶ **Solve Numeric Percent Problems**

14. What is 25% of 32?

$$\text{Part} \quad \frac{25}{100} = \frac{\square}{32}$$
$$\text{Whole}$$
Percent Number

Why do we write $\frac{25}{100}$?

_____

Why is 32 in the denominator?

_____

Solve by simplifying: $\frac{25}{100} = \frac{\square}{\square} = \frac{\square}{32}$

15. 27 is 30% of what?

$$\text{Part} \quad \frac{30}{100} = \frac{27}{\square}$$
$$\text{Whole}$$
Percent Number

Why do we write $\frac{30}{100}$?

_____

Why is 27 in the numerator?

_____

Solve by simplifying: $\frac{30}{100} = \frac{\square}{\square} = \frac{27}{\square}$

16. 21 is what percent of 28?

$$\text{Part} \quad \frac{\square}{100} = \frac{21}{28}$$
$$\text{Whole}$$
Percent Number

Why is the unknown number above 100?

_____

Why is 21 above 28?

_____

Solve by simplifying: $\frac{21}{28} = \frac{\square}{\square} =$

17. What is 125% of 28?

$$\text{Part} \quad \frac{125}{100} = \frac{\square}{28}$$
$$\text{Whole}$$
Percent Number

Why is the part greater than the whole?

_____

Why is 28 in the denominator?

_____

Will the unknown number be greater than or less than 28? Why?

_____

Solve by simplifying: $\frac{125}{100} = \frac{\square}{\square} = \frac{\square}{28}$

Set up a proportion and solve by simplifying and finding an equivalent fraction.

18. 75% of 24 is _____.

19. 28 is 80% of _____.

20. 9 is _____ % of 36.

21. 140% of 30 is _____.

UNIT 6 LESSON 11   CA Standards: KEY NS 1.2; MR 2.3   Solve Problems Using Percents **421**

Solve Word Problems

Solve the word problems using any method.

22. In Mr. Roberts's class there are 30 children. 18 of them are girls. What percent of the children in Mr. Roberts's class are girls?

23. Andrew counted 20 fish in the pond at City Park. 15 were goldfish and the rest were carp. What percent of the fish were goldfish?

24. A jug holds 80 mL of water when it is full. How much water will there be in the jug when it is 75% full?

25. After a long diet, the dog Lucky weighed 54 pounds. That was 90% of his old weight. How much did Lucky weigh before the diet?

26. Emma saw the movie *The Mummy* 4 times. That is only 80% of the number of times Yoko has seen it. How many times has Yoko seen *The Mummy*?

27. Kevin made 55 sandwiches for the party. 33 of the sandwiches were tuna. What percent of the sandwiches were tuna?

28. Chip has already eaten 320 of the 400 acorns he collected for winter. What percent of his acorns has Chip eaten?

29. In Mr. Smith's front yard there is an olive tree and a palm tree. The olive tree is 12 feet tall and the palm tree is 15 feet tall. The olive tree's height is what percent of the palm tree's height?

6-12 Class Activity

▶ Solve Probability Problems

Solve each problem using any method.

Show your work.

1. A box of 40 crayons has 10 shades of red, 6 shades of blue, 4 shades of yellow, 2 shades of purple, as well as other colors. What is the probability of getting a red crayon? A blue crayon? A yellow crayon? A purple crayon? Express your answers as a percent.

2. The grab bag at the town picnic contained 2,000 tickets to local baseball games. 40% were Pigeon tickets, 35% were Robin tickets, and 25% were Sparrow tickets. If you drew out 20 tickets, how many tickets for each team would you expect to get? How many Pigeon tickets are there?

3. Peppy the cat sleeps 18 hours a day. What is the percent chance that you will find Peppy asleep at any one time of day?

4. A bushel of apples contains 32 Jonathan apples, 28 Golden Delicious apples, and 20 Granny Smith apples. What are your chances of picking one Jonathan apple from the bushel? Express your answer as a percent.

5. What are your chances of each spinner landing on a dark space? Express your answers as a percent.

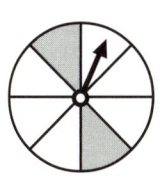
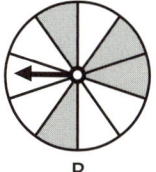

A   B

Name _____ **Date** _____

6. Of the 5,000 children who live in Garden Town, 4,500 love to eat vegetables.

   What percent of the children love to eat vegetables?

   _____

7. Of the 30 children who live on Green Bean Street in Garden Town, how many probably do not like to eat vegetables?

   _____

8. A box of 30 chocolates has 12 chocolate-covered caramels, 6 chocolate-covered cherries, 3 chocolates with nougat centers, and 9 solid chocolates. What is the probability of picking a chocolate-covered caramel? A chocolate-covered cherry? A chocolate with a nougat center? Solid chocolate? Express your answers as percents.

   _____

   _____

   _____

9. Dorothy bought a bag of 500 mixed flower seeds. The bag contained 250 dahlia seeds, 120 daisy seeds, 75 violet seeds, and the rest were forget-me-nots. Dorothy planted 200 of the seeds in her garden. How many of each flower can she expect to grow in her garden?

   _____

   _____

Name _____ Date _____

1. Circle the multiplication column table. Explain why the other table is not a multiplication column table.

0	0
1	3
2	6
3	8
4	10
5	13
6	17
7	18

0	0
1	8
2	16
3	24
4	32
5	40
6	48
7	56

_____

_____

_____

2. Grandma Jackson has 35 tomato plants in 7 rows of her garden. Complete this statement.

   Grandma Jackson has

   _____ per _____.

3. Make a ratio table for this situation.

   A fruit salad recipe calls for 7 bananas for every 3 oranges.

   Be sure to label your table.

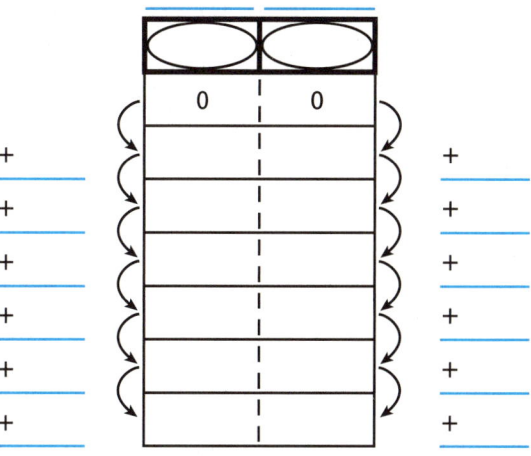

Ratio Table

4. What is the value of n?

   $n : 27 = 14 : 18$

   $n =$ _____

UNIT 6 TEST

Complete the Factor Puzzle and solve the problem.

5. Jerry saved $12 for every $15 that Ellen saved. When Jerry had saved $28, how much had Ellen saved?

   _____

Solve each problem.

Show your work.

6. Janet drives 10 miles in 16 minutes. How long does it take her to drive 45 miles at the same rate?

   _____

7. Every day during October, Ms. Carter fills 3 baskets with apples and 8 baskets with pears. When she has 40 baskets of pears, how many baskets of apples does she have?

   _____

8. Al had $75 when he went shopping. He spent 60% of his money. How much money did he have left when he came home?

   _____

9. A bag of 25 marbles contains 8 red marbles. If one marble is picked from the bag, what is the probability that it is red? Express your answer as a percent.

   _____

10. **Extended Response** Write a word problem for the proportion and show how to solve the problem.

    $$n : 35 = 18 : 42$$

    _____

    _____

    _____

    _____

426 UNIT 6 TEST

Name   Date

UNIT F LESSON 1   Similar Figures **427**

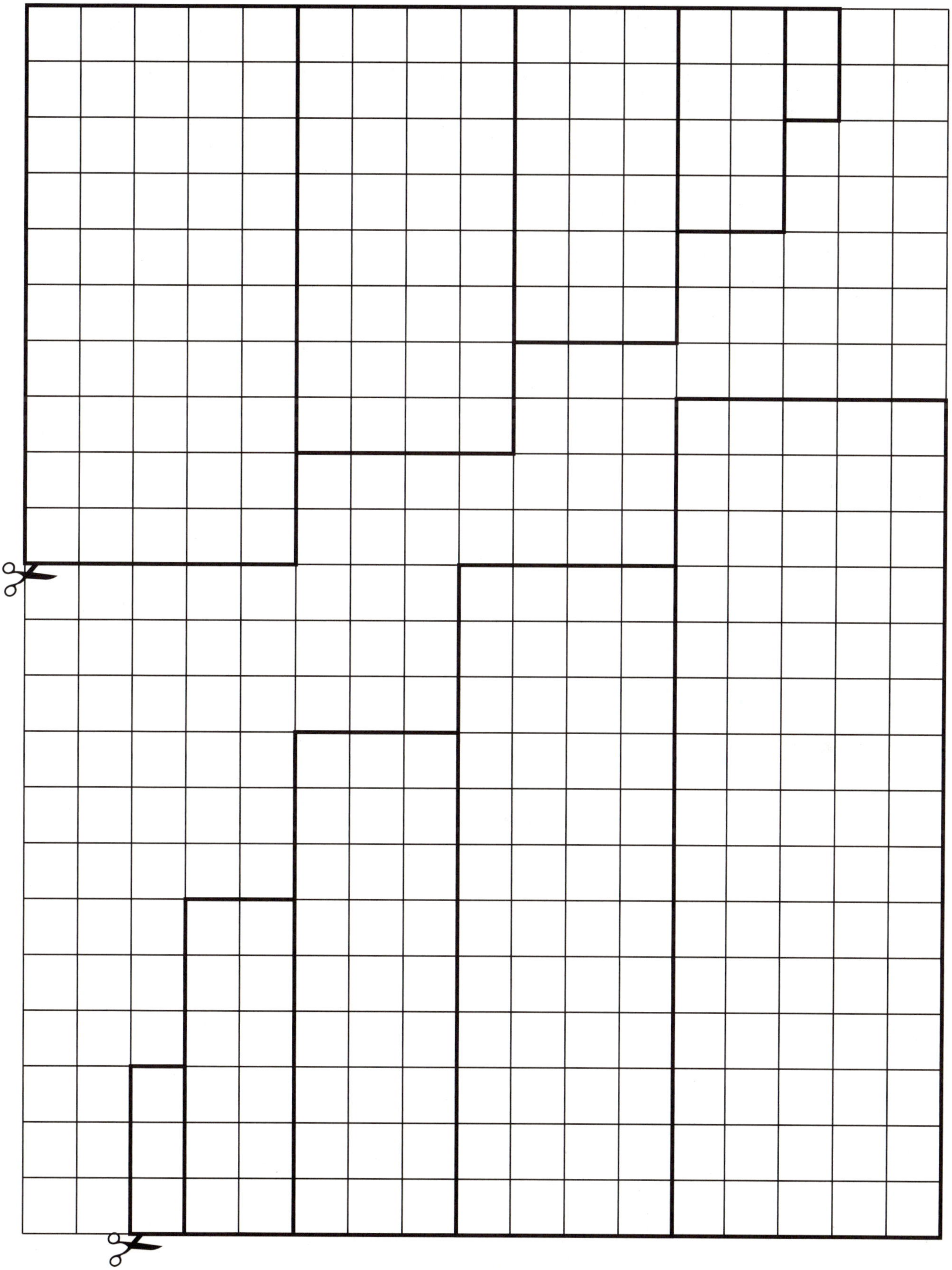

Class Activity

▶ Discuss Similar Figures

Vocabulary
similar
ratio

When figures are **similar**, the measures of corresponding angles are equal and the lengths of corresponding sides are proportional: they share the same **ratio**.

All of these rectangles are similar.

Two of these triangles are similar.

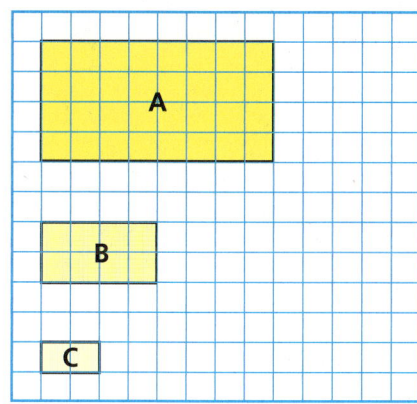
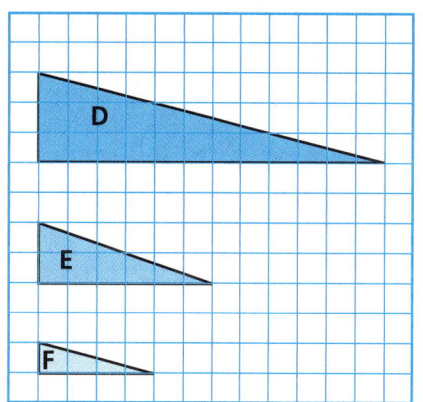

1. Write a ratio $b : h$ that compares the lengths of the base and the height.

   A _____ B _____ C _____

2. Write a ratio $b : h$ that compares the lengths of the base and the height. Circle the similar triangles.

   D _____ E _____ F _____

Is each pair of figures similar? Circle yes or no. Show why or why not with ratios.

3.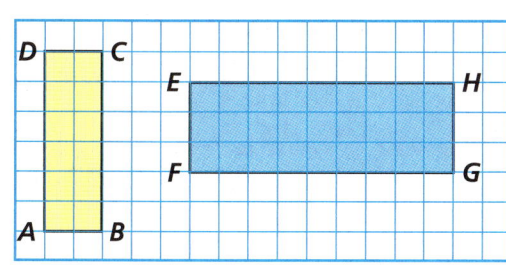

   yes
   no _____

4.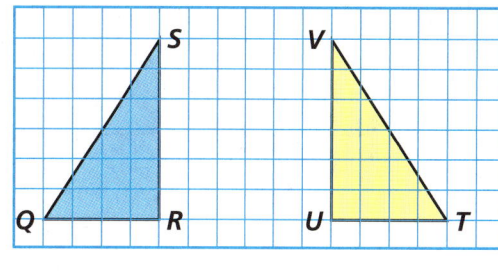

   yes
   no _____

5.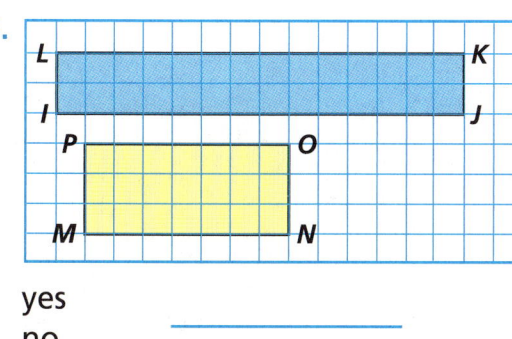

   yes
   no _____

6.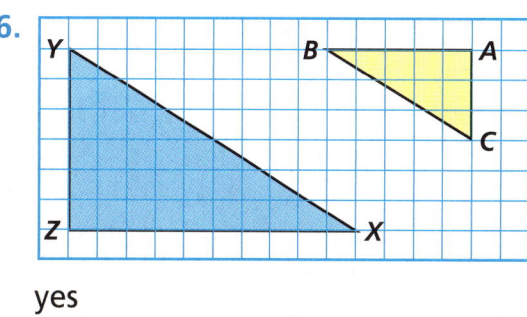

   yes
   no _____

UNIT F LESSON 1

Similar Figures **429**

▶ Rotating and Reflecting

Sometimes you need to rotate or reflect similar figures to find the corresponding sides to make ratios.

Write the ratios from these similar figures in a Factor Puzzle to find each unknown side.

1.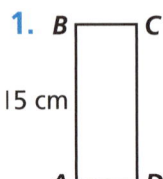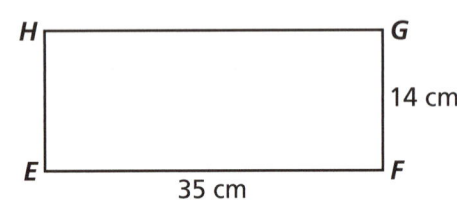

2.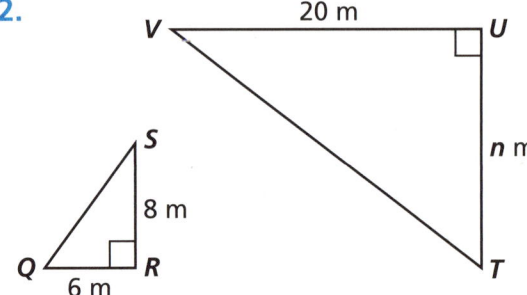

$\overline{AD} : \overline{FG}$

$\overline{AB} :$ _____

$\overline{AD} =$ _____

_____

_____

$\overline{UT} =$ _____

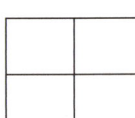

3.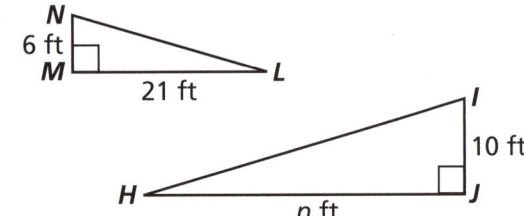

4.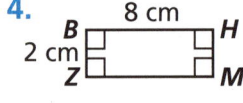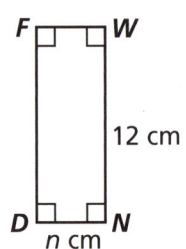

_____

_____

$\overline{HJ} =$ _____

_____

_____

$\overline{FW} =$ _____

Anna and Fumi want to know how tall the school flagpole is. They have a stick that is 8 feet long. Discuss these questions about how they can use the stick and shadows to answer their question.

- What is true about the lengths of the objects and their shadows?
- Does it matter how high the sun is in the sky?
- If the shadow of the flagpole is 7 ft long and the shadow of the stick is 2 ft long, how tall is the flagpole?

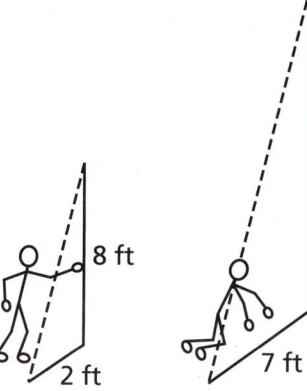

Solve. Use what you know about similar triangles.

1. Two students measure their shadows on a sunny day. The student who is 63 in. tall has a shadow of 35 in. How tall is the student whose shadow is 30 in. long?

2. Joshua and Erin measure the shadows made by their houses. Joshua's house has a 30-foot shadow and Erin's has a 35-foot shadow. Erin knows that her house is 21 ft tall. How tall is Joshua's house?

3. The shorter statue in the park has a height of 12 feet and a shadow of 15 feet. The shadow of the taller statue is 30 feet long. What is the height of the taller statue?

4. Two buildings have shadows that are the same length. What is true about their heights?

5. Martha's height is 5 ft, 2 inches. She is twice as tall as her 2-year-old sister. Her sister's shadow is 3 feet long. How long is Martha's shadow?

UNIT F LESSON 1

Similar Figures **431**

F–1 Going Further

Name _______________ Date _______________

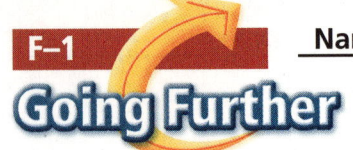

▶ Show Perspective

Similarity can be used to show perspective. The smaller a figure is, the farther away it appears. The small rectangle represents a rectangle that is the same size as the big rectangle. It is just farther away.

1. To show perspective, use your ruler to draw lines to connect corresponding vertices on the similar rectangles.

2. Find other rectangles that fit within the lines you drew. Put their bases and heights in the table. Some may have fractional bases and heights.

b* : *h
8 : 4
6 : 3
5 : $2\frac{1}{2}$
4 : 2
2 : 1

Dear Family,

In this unit, your child is introduced to similarity and scale. There are two main goals for this unit:

1. Students will identify and draw similar figures, and use similarity to find a missing measurement.

   - One figure is similar to another if it has the same shape. It may be enlarged or reduced.
   - In similar figures, the measurements of corresponding angles are equal and the lengths of the sides share the same ratio.

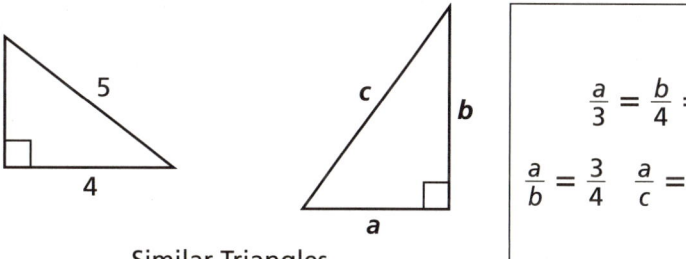

Similar Triangles

A Factor Puzzle can be used to find an unknown length in a similarity problem.

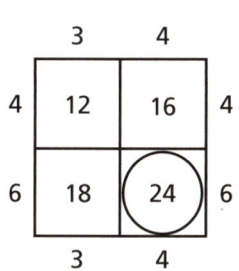

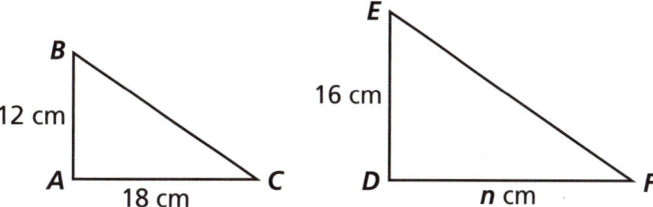

For these similar triangles, students can make and solve the Factor Puzzle shown in the margin to find that the unknown length is 24 cm.

2. Students will analyze and interpret scale drawings, including maps, and make two-dimensional scale drawings.

   - In scale drawings and maps, the actual object and the drawing are similar.
   - The scale tells the relationship between the distances in the drawing or map and the actual distances. For example, $\frac{1}{4}$ inch = 100 miles means that every $\frac{1}{4}$ inch on the map represents 100 actual miles.

If you have any questions or comments, please call or write to me.

Sincerely,
Your child's teacher

Estimada familia:

En esta unidad su niño empieza a estudiar la semejanza y las escalas. Esta unidad tiene dos objetivos principales:

1. Los estudiantes identificarán y dibujarán figuras semejantes y usarán la semejanza para hallar una medida que falta.

- Una figura es semejante a otra si tiene la misma forma. El tamaño de la figura puede aumentar o disminuir.

- En figuras semejantes, las medidas de los ángulos correspondientes son iguales y las longitudes de los lados tienen la misma razón.

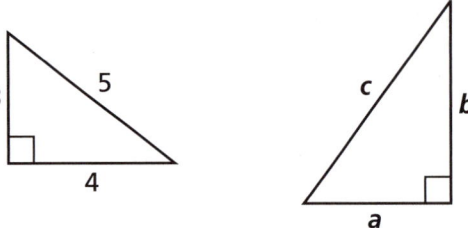 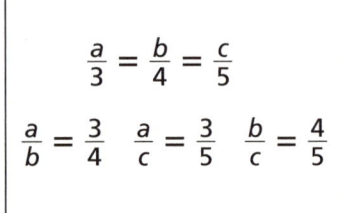

Triángulos semejantes

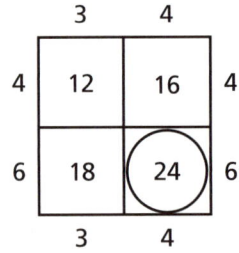

Se puede usar un rompecabezas de factores para hallar una longitud desconocida en un problema de semejanza.

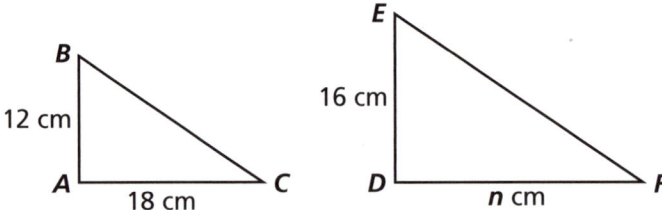

Para estos triángulos semejantes, los estudiantes pueden hacer y resolver el rompecabezas de factores que se muestra en el margen y determinar que la longitud desconocida es 24 cm.

2. Los estudiantes analizarán e interpretarán dibujos a escala y mapas, y harán dibujos bidimensionales a escala.

- En los dibujos a escala y en los mapas, el objeto real y el dibujo son semejantes.

- La escala indica la relación entre las distancias en el dibujo o mapa y las distancias reales. Por ejemplo: $\frac{1}{4}$ de pulgada = 100 millas significa que cada $\frac{1}{4}$ de pulgada del mapa representa 100 millas reales.

Si tiene alguna duda o comentario, por favor comuníquese conmigo.

Atentamente,
El maestro de su niño

F-2 Class Activity

Name _____ Date _____

Vocabulary
scale drawing
scale

▶ **Read a Map**

A map is an example of a **scale drawing**. On the map below, every inch represents a specified distance. To find the distance that an inch represents, use the **scale** located on the map.

1. What distance does each inch on the map represent?

   _____

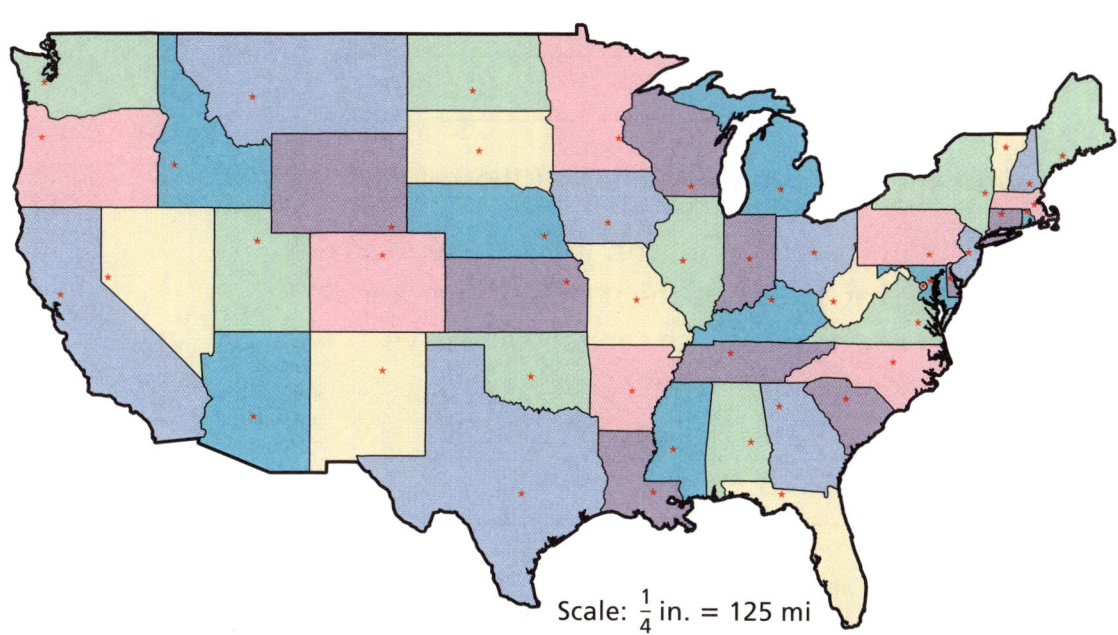

Scale: $\frac{1}{4}$ in. = 125 mi

Use the map and an inch ruler to answer the questions below.

2. Choose a state capital and write its name.

   _____

3. Locate another state capital and write its name.

   _____

4. To the nearest fifty miles, what is the distance between the capitals? _____ miles

Class Activity

▶ Plan a Trip

Use the map on the previous page and an inch ruler to answer the questions below.

5. List four states you might like to visit someday.

   _____
   _____
   _____
   _____

6. On the map, write the names of the capitals of those states.

7. Plan a trip to visit those capitals. Your trip should begin and end at your own state capital. Write the names of the capitals in the order you will visit them. Which capital will you visit first? Which will you visit second?

   _____
   _____

8. Using the map scale and an inch ruler, estimate the total distance you will travel, to the nearest hundred miles.

   _____ miles

9. If you change the order in which you visit the capitals, will the total distance of your trip change? Explain.

   _____
   _____

10. In which order should you visit the capitals so that your trip is the shortest possible distance? What is that distance?

    _____
    _____

Class Activity

▶ Will It Fit?

Vocabulary
scale drawing

In a **scale drawing**, the scale tells how the measurements in the drawing relate to the actual measurements.

Use a centimeter ruler to measure the rugs in exercises 1 and 2. Then decide if each rug will fit in your classroom. Write yes or no.

1. To the right is a view of a rug drawn to the scale 1 cm = 60 cm.

   _____

   1 cm = 60 cm

2. This is a view of a different rug drawn to the scale 1 cm = 2 m.

   _____

   1 cm = 2 m

3. If the scale in exercise 2 were changed to 1 cm = 1 m, how would the size of the actual rug change? Explain your answer.

   _____
   _____
   _____
   _____

UNIT F LESSON 3   Explore Scale Drawings **437**

Name _____ Date _____

▶ Draw to Scale

Choose an object in your classroom with a rectangular shape, such as your desktop or a window. Use the quarter-inch grid below to make a scale drawing of the object. Include the scale.

Name _____ Date _____

Vocabulary
floor plan

▶ **Discuss a Floor Plan**

When interior designers draw a **floor plan** of a room, they often suggest where furniture should be placed. The floor plan below is a scale drawing of a room.

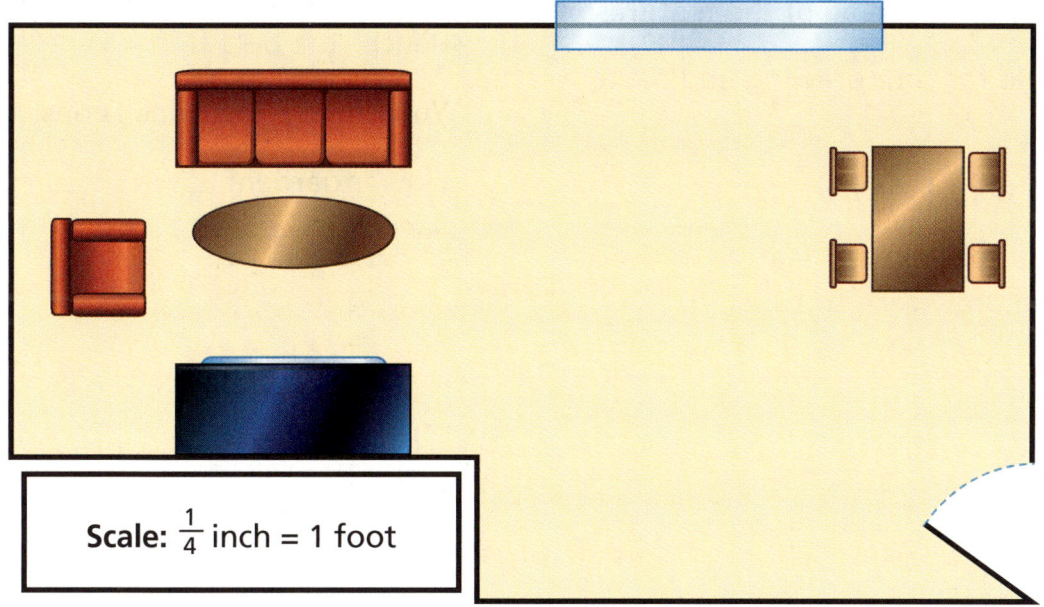

Scale: $\frac{1}{4}$ inch = 1 foot

Use your inch ruler and the scale to answer the questions below.

1. What is the length of the actual sofa? _____

2. What is the length of the actual armchair? _____

3. How much floor space does the actual dining room table take up? _____

4. About how far from the actual sofa is the TV? _____

5. How wide is the actual window? _____

6. Explain why you cannot determine the height of the window.

   _____

7. Draw a bookshelf in the room. What is the width and the depth of the bookshelf you drew? What is its actual width and actual depth?

   _____

   _____

UNIT F LESSON 4   Use Scale Drawings **439**

Class Activity

▶ **Make a Scale Drawing**

The table on the right describes a backyard and its features.

On the grid below, make a scale drawing of the backyard and include all of the features.

- Choose a scale for your drawing and make a key.
- Draw the border of the backyard.
- Choose a location for each feature in the backyard and draw each to scale.

Actual Dimensions

Yard: 400 sq ft
Patio: 10 ft by 12 ft
Picnic table: 4 ft by 6 ft
Children's pool: 4 ft in diameter
Bench: 1 ft by 3 ft

You Choose the Dimensions

Flower garden: _____
Sandbox: _____

440 UNIT F LESSON 4 — Use Scale Drawings

Name _____ Date _____

Is each pair of figures similar? Circle yes or no.

1.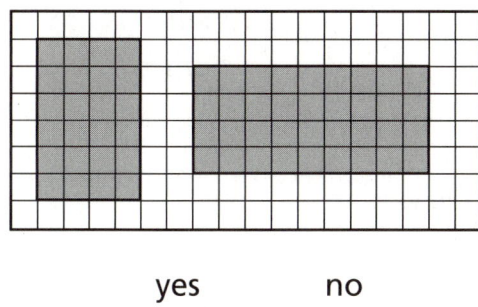

    yes   no

2.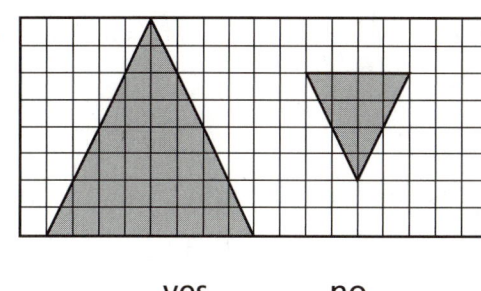

    yes   no

3. Draw a similar triangle with sides twice as long as the given triangle.

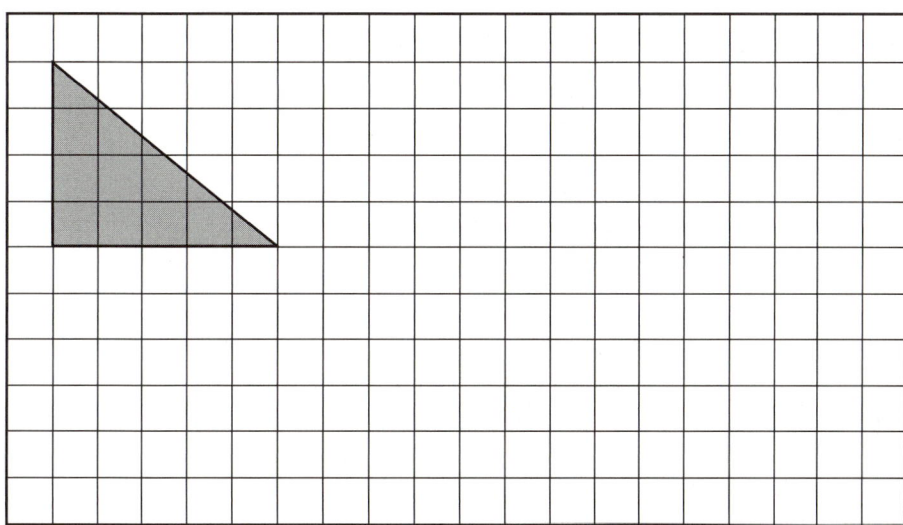

4. Write the missing measurement.

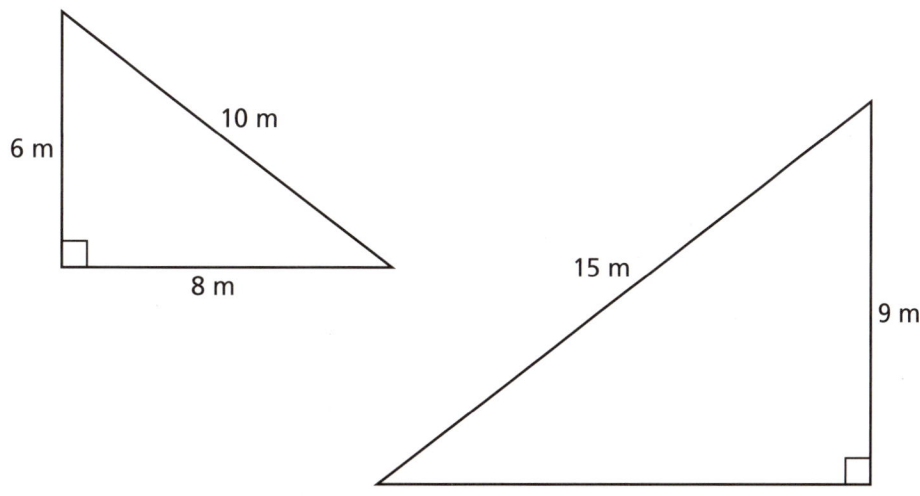

_____

UNIT F TEST   441

Name _____ Date _____

Use the scale to solve for *n*. Show your work.

5. 1 in. = 5 ft
   4 in. = *n* ft
   _____

6. $\frac{1}{2}$ in. = 1 mi
   $3\frac{1}{2}$ in. = *n* mi
   _____

7. 1 cm = 3 km
   n cm = 7.5 km
   _____

8. This scale drawing shows that the distance from Orrville to Beetown is 60 km. What is the distance from Orrville to King City?

   _____

   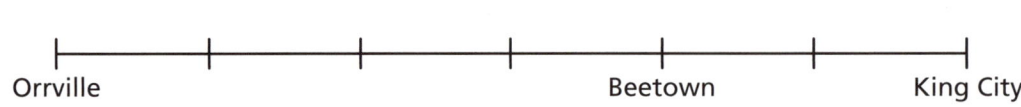

   Orrville   Beetown   King City

9. On a map, the distance between two cities is 7 in. The real distance is 21 mi. What distance does 1 in. represent on the map?

   _____

10. **Extended Response** Make a scale drawing of a rug that measures 9 feet by 12 feet. Include a key.

442 UNIT F TEST

Glossary

A

acre A measure of land area. An acre is equal to 4,840 square yards.

acute angle An angle whose measure is less than 90°.

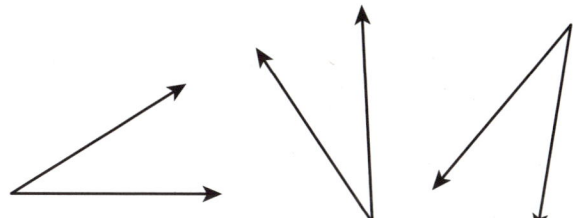

acute triangle A triangle with three acute angles.

addend One of two or more numbers added together to find a sum.

Example:

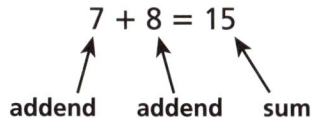

Add On Method for Subtraction Find the difference between two numbers by adding to the lesser number to get the greater number.

angle A figure formed by two rays or line segments with a common endpoint.

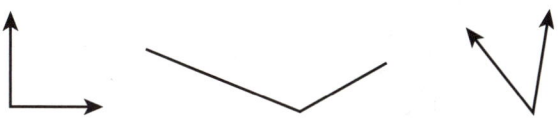

apex The vertex of a cone.

area The amount of surface covered by a figure measured in square units.

array An arrangement of objects, symbols, or numbers in equal rows and equal columns.

Associative Property of Addition Changing the grouping of addends does not change the sum.

Example:
$3 + (5 + 7) = (3 + 5) + 7$

Associative Property of Multiplication Changing the grouping of factors does not change the product.

Example:
$3 \times (5 \times 7) = (3 \times 5) \times 7$

average (See **mean**)

axis A line, usually horizontal or vertical, that is labeled with numbers or words to show the meaning of a graph.

B

bar graph A graph that uses bars to show data.

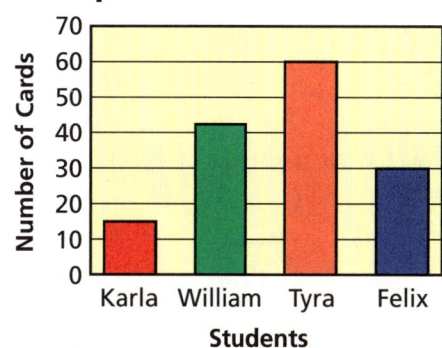

Glossary (Continued)

base For a triangle or parallelogram, a base is any side. For a trapezoid, a base is either of the parallel sides. For a prism, a base is one of the congruent parallel faces. For a pyramid, the base is the face that does not touch the vertex of the pyramid.

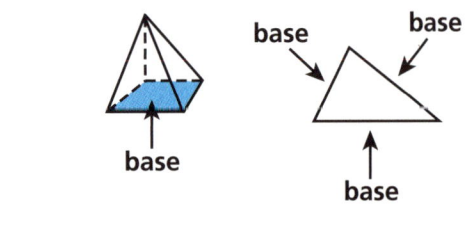

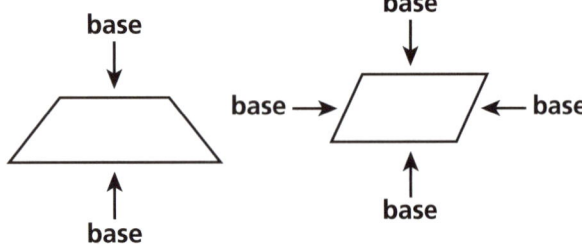

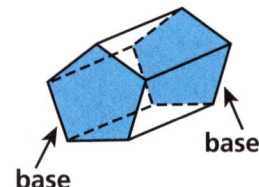

billion One thousand million.
1,000,000,000

billionth One thousandth of a millionth.
0.000000001

C

capacity A measure of how much a container can hold.

Celsius The metric temperature scale.

centimeter A unit of measure in the metric system that equals one hundredth of a meter. 1 cm = 0.01 m

1 cm

change minus A change situation that can be represented by subtraction. In a change minus situation, the starting number, the change, or the result will be unknown.

Example:
Unknown Start	Unknown Change	Unknown Result
$n - 2 = 3$	$5 - n = 3$	$5 - 2 = n$

change plus A change situation that can be represented by addition. In a change plus situation, the starting number, the change, or the result will be unknown.

Example:
Unknown Start	Unknown Change	Unknown Result
$n + 2 = 5$	$3 + n = 5$	$3 + 2 = n$

circle A plane figure that forms a closed path so that all the points on the path are the same distance from a point called the center.

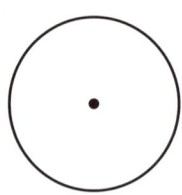

circle graph A graph that uses parts of a circle to show data.

Zak's Book Collection

circumference The distance around a circle.

collection situations Situations that involve putting together (joining) or taking apart (separating) groups.

column A part of a table or array that contains items arranged vertically.

⋮

combination situation A combination situation is one in which pairs or sets are counted. Tables can be used to show combinations.

Types of Sandwiches			
	Cheese	Peanut Butter	Tuna
White	W + C	W + PB	W + T
Wheat	Wh + C	Wh + PB	Wh + T

common denominator A common multiple of two or more denominators.

Example: 6 could be used as a common denominator for $\frac{1}{2}$ and $\frac{1}{3}$.

$$\frac{1}{2} = \frac{3}{6} \qquad \frac{1}{3} = \frac{2}{6}$$

so $\frac{1}{2} + \frac{1}{3} = \frac{3}{6} + \frac{2}{6} = \frac{5}{6}$

Commutative Property of Addition Changing the order of addends does not change the sum.

Example: $3 + 8 = 8 + 3$

Commutative Property of Multiplication Changing the order of factors does not change the product.

Example: $3 \times 8 = 8 \times 3$

comparison situation A situation in which two amounts are compared by addition or by multiplication. An additive comparison situation compares by asking or telling how much more (how much less) one amount is than another. A multiplicative comparison situation compares by asking or telling how many times as many one amount is as another. The multiplicative comparison may also be made using fraction language. For example, you can say, "Sally has one fourth as much as Tom has," instead of saying "Tom has 4 times as much as Sally has."

complementary angles Angles having a sum of 90°.

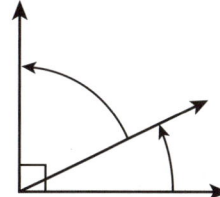

complex figure A figure made by combining simple geometric figures like rectangles and triangles.

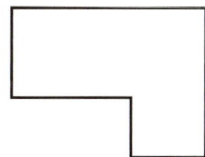 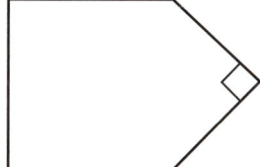

composite number A number greater than 1 that has more than one factor pair. Examples of composite numbers are 4, 15, and 45. The factor pairs of 15 are: 1 and 15, 3 and 5.

Glossary (Continued)

cone A solid figure with a curved base and a single vertex.

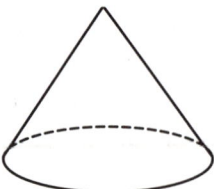

congruent Exactly the same size and shape.

Example: Triangles ABC and PQR are congruent.

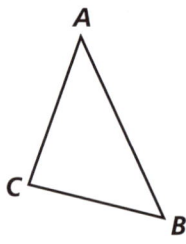 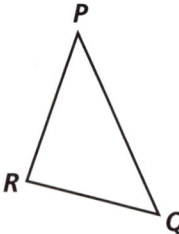

coordinate A number that determines the position of a point in one direction on a grid.

counterexample An example that proves that a general statement is false.

cube A solid figure that has 6 faces that are congruent squares.

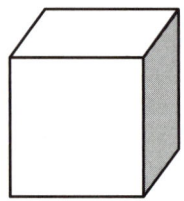

cubic centimeter A metric unit for measuring volume. It is the volume of a cube with one-centimeter edges.

cubic meter A metric unit for measuring volume. It is the volume of a cube with one-meter edges.

cubic unit A unit of volume made by a cube with all edges one unit long.

Example: Cubic centimeters and cubic inches are cubic units.

cup A U.S. customary unit of capacity equal to half a pint.

D

data Pieces of information.

decimal number A representation of a number using the numerals 0 to 9, in which each digit has a value 10 times the digit to its right. A dot or decimal point separates the whole-number part of the number on the left from the fractional part on the right.

decimeter A unit of measure in the metric system that equals one tenth of a meter. 1 dm = 0.1 m

degree A unit for measuring angles. Also a unit for measuring temperature. (See Celsius and Fahrenheit.)

denominator The number below the bar in a fraction. It tells the number of unit fractions into which the 1 whole is divided.

Example: 4 is the denominator.

diagonal A line segment connecting two vertices that are not next to each other.

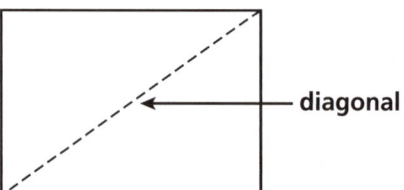

S4 Glossary

diameter A line segment from one side of a circle to the other through the center. Also the length of that segment.

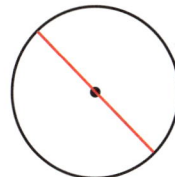

difference The result of a subtraction.

Example: 54 − 37 = 17
                        ↑— difference

digit Any of the symbols 0, 1, 2, 3, 4, 5, 6, 7, 8, or 9.

Digit-by-Digit A method used to solve a division problem.

Example:

```
            Put in only
            one digit at
            a time.
            5 ↙              54              546
         7)3,822          7)3,822         7)3,822
         − 3 5            − 3 5           − 3 5
         ─────            ─────           ─────
           32               32              32
                          − 28            − 28
                          ─────           ─────
                            42              42
                                         − 42
                                         ─────
```

dimension The height, length, or width.

Examples:

A line segment has only length, so it has *one* dimension.

A rectangle has length and width, so it has *two* dimensions.

A cube has length, width, and height, so it has *three* dimensions.

Distributive Property You can multiply a sum by a number, or multiply each addend by the number and add the products; the result is the same.

Example:
$3 \times (2 + 4) = (3 \times 2) + (3 \times 4)$
$3 \times 6 \ = \ 6 \ + \ 12$
$18 \ = \ 18$

divisible A number is divisible by another number if the quotient is a whole number with no remainder.

Example: 15 is divisible by 5 because 15 ÷ 5 = 3

dot array An arrangement of dots in rows and columns.

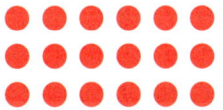

double bar graph Data is compared by using pairs of bars drawn next to each other.

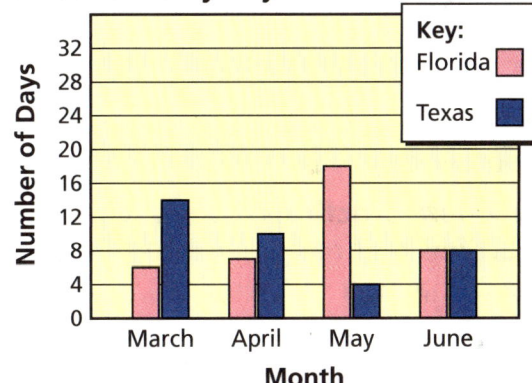

E

edge A line segment that forms as a side of a two-dimensional figure or the part of a three-dimensional figure where two faces meet.

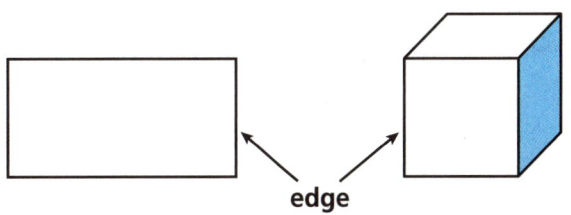

Glossary (Continued)

elapsed time The amount of time that passes between two times.

equal groups Groups that have the same number of objects.

 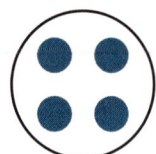 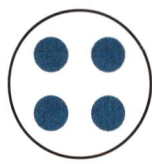

equation A statement that two expressions are equal. An equation always has an equals sign.

Example: $32 + 35 = 67$
$50 = 75 - 25$
$1 + 10 + 40 = 53 - 2$

equilateral Having all equal sides.

Example: An equilateral triangle

equivalent Representing the same number or amount.

equivalent fractions Two or more fractions that represent the same fractional part of 1 whole.

estimate Find *about* how many or *about* how much. A reasonable guess about a measurement or answer.

even number A whole number that is a multiple of 2. An even number ends with a 0, 2, 4, 6, or 8.

Example: 68 is an even number because it is a multiple of 2; $2 \times 34 = 68$.

example A specific instance that demonstrates a general statement.

expanded form A way of writing a number that shows the value of each of its digits.

Example: Expanded form of 835:
$800 + 30 + 5$
8 hundreds + 3 tens + 5 ones

Expanded Notation A strategy used to solve multiplication and division problems.

67×43

$43 = 40 + 3$
$\times\ 67 = 60 + 7$

$60 \times 40 = 2{,}400$
$60 \times\ \ 3 =\ \ \ 180$
$\ \ 7 \times 40 =\ \ \ 280$
$\ \ 7 \times\ \ 3 =\ \ \ \ \ 21$
$\ \ \ \ \ \ \ \ \ \ \ \ \ \ \ 2{,}881$

$\ \ \ 43$
$\times\ 67$
$2{,}400$
$\ \ 180$
$\ \ 280$
$\ \ \ \ 21$
$2{,}881$

$3{,}822 \div 7$

Show the zeros in the places.

$\ \ \ \ \ \ \ 500$
$7\overline{)3{,}822}$
$-3{,}500$
$\ \ \ \ \ 322$

$\ \ \ \ \ \ \ \ 40$
$\ \ \ \ \ \ 500$
$7\overline{)3{,}822}$
$-3{,}500$
$\ \ \ \ \ 322$
$-\ 280$
$\ \ \ \ \ \ 42$

$\ \ \ \ \ \ \ \ \ 6$
$\ \ \ \ \ \ \ 40\ \ )546$
$\ \ \ \ \ \ 500$
$7\overline{)3{,}822}$
$-3{,}500$
$\ \ \ \ \ 322$
$-\ 280$
$\ \ \ \ \ \ 42$
$-\ \ 42$

expression A combination of one or more numbers, variables, or numbers and variables with one or more operations.

Examples: 4
$6n$
$6n - 5$
$7 + 4$
$2(3 + 4)$

F

face A flat surface of a three-dimensional figure.

factor One of two or more numbers multiplied together to make a product.
Example:

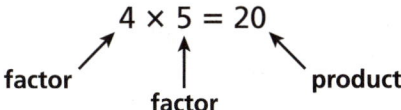

Factor Puzzle A two-by-two table that is made from the cells in two rows and two columns of the Multiplication Table. It can be used to solve proportions. The unknown number in the ○ will be 5 × 3 = 15.

```
      3   7
    ┌───┬───┐
  2 │ 6 │14 │ 2
    ├───┼───┤
  5 │ ○ │35 │ 5
    └───┴───┘
      3   7
```

Fahrenheit The temperature scale used in the United States. Water freezes at 32°F and boils at 212°F.

floor plan A scale drawing of a room as seen from above.

foot A U.S. customary unit of length equal to 12 inches and $\frac{1}{3}$ yard.

fraction A number that is the sum of unit fractions, each an equal part of a set or part of a whole.
Examples: $\frac{3}{4} = \frac{1}{4} + \frac{1}{4} + \frac{1}{4}$
$\frac{5}{4} = \frac{1}{4} + \frac{1}{4} + \frac{1}{4} + \frac{1}{4} + \frac{1}{4}$

function A consistent relationship between two sets of numbers. Each number in one of the sets is paired with exactly one number in the other set. A function can be shown in a chart, or as a set of ordered pairs.

Example: The relationship between the number of yards and the number of feet.

$f = 3y$

Yards	1	2	3	4	5	6	7
Feet	3	6	9	12	15	18	21

G

gallon A U.S. customary unit of capacity equal to 4 quarts, 8 pints, and 16 cups.

gram The basic unit of mass in the metric system.

greater than (>) A symbol used when comparing two numbers. The greater number is given first.
Example: 33 > 17
33 is greater than 17.

greatest Largest.

H

half turn A 180° rotation.

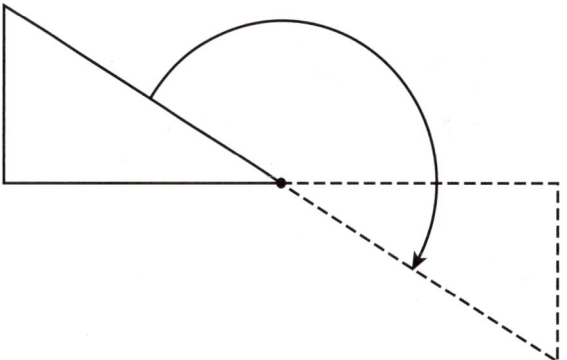

height The perpendicular distance from a base of a figure to the highest point.

Glossary (Continued)

hexagon A six-sided polygon.

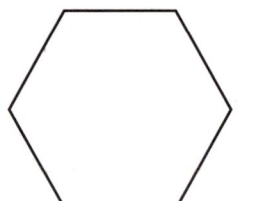 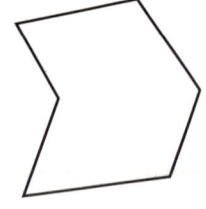

histogram A graph in which bars are used to display how frequently data occurs between intervals.

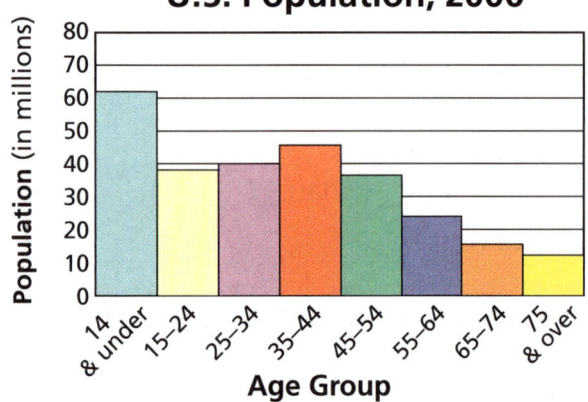

I

Identity Property of Multiplication The product of 1 and any number equals that number.

Example: $10 \times 1 = 10$

improper fraction A fraction whose numerator is greater than or equal to the denominator.

Example: $\frac{3}{2}$

inch A U.S. customary unit of length. There are 12 inches in 1 foot.

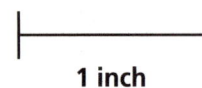
1 inch

inequality A statement that two expressions are not equal.

Examples: $2 < 5$
$4 + 5 > 12 - 8$

inverse operations Opposite or reverse operations that undo each other. Addition and subtraction are inverse operations. Multiplication and division are inverse operations.

Examples: $4 + 6 = 10$, so $10 - 6 = 4$
$3 \times 9 = 27$, so $27 \div 9 = 3$

isosceles trapezoid A trapezoid with one pair of opposite congruent sides.

isosceles triangle A triangle with at least two congruent sides.

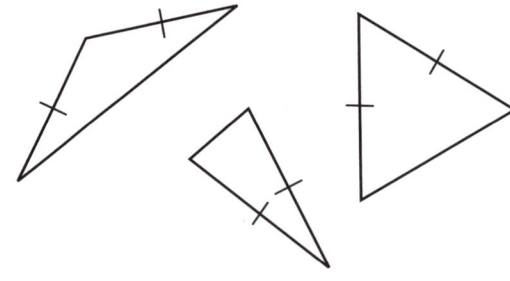

K

key A part of a map, graph, or chart that explains what symbols mean.

kilogram A unit of mass in the metric system that equals one thousand grams. 1 kg = 1,000 g

kiloliter A unit of capacity in the metric system that equals one thousand liters. 1 kL = 1,000 L

kilometer A unit of length in the metric system that equals one thousand meters. 1 km = 1,000 m

L

least Smallest.

least common denominator The least common multiple of two denominators.
Example: 6 is the least common denominator of $\frac{1}{2}$ and $\frac{1}{3}$.

length The measure of a line segment, or of one side or edge of a figure.

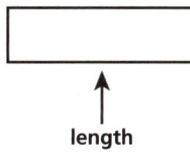
length

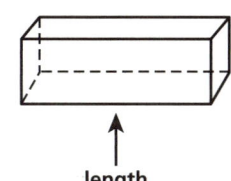
length

less than (<) A symbol used when comparing two numbers. The smaller number is given first.
Example: 54 < 78
54 is less than 78.

line A straight path that goes on forever in opposite directions.
Example: line AB

line graph A graph that uses a broken line to show changes in data.

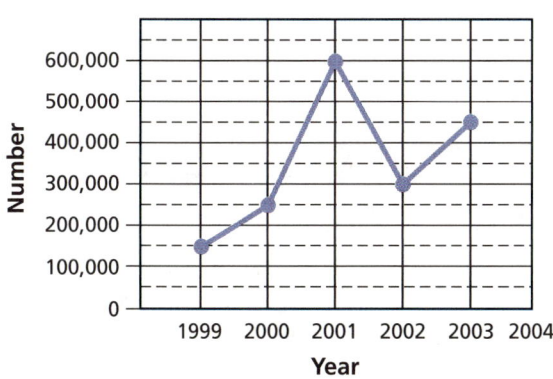

line plot A diagram that shows the frequency of data on a number line.

line of symmetry A line such that if a figure is folded on that line, the two parts will match exactly.

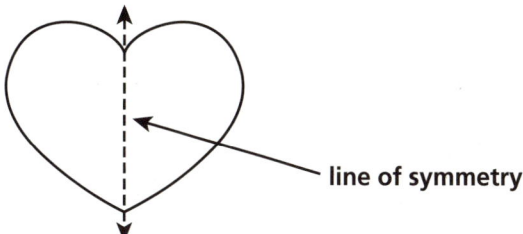
line of symmetry

line segment Part of a line that has two endpoints.

line symmetry A figure has line symmetry if it can be folded along a line to create two halves that match exactly.

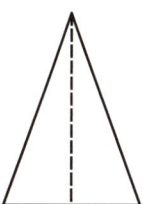

Linked Multiplication Column Table A Multiplication Column Table that also has a column showing the unit that links the terms in each ratio.
Example: This table shows the ratios of two rates, $3 per day and $5 per day, and the linking unit, days.

Days	Noreen ③	Tim ⑤
0	0	0
1	3	5
2	6	10
3	9	15
4	12	20

Glossary (Continued)

liter The basic unit of capacity in the metric system.

M

mass The measure of the amount of matter in an object.

mean (average) The mean is the size of each of n equal groups made from n data values. The mean can be found by adding the values in a set of data and dividing by the number of such values.

Example: 75, 84, 89, 91, 101
75 + 84 + 89 + 91 + 101 = 440,
then 440 ÷ 5 = 88. The mean is 88.

measure of central tendency The mean, median, or mode of a set of numbers.

median The middle number in a set of ordered numbers. For an even number of numbers, the median is the number halfway between the two middle numbers.

Examples: 13 26 34 47 52
The median for this set is 34.
8 8 12 14 20 21
The median for this set is 13.

meter The basic unit of length in the metric system.

milligram A unit of mass in the metric system that equals one thousandth of a gram. 1 mg = 0.001 g

milliliter A unit of capacity in the metric system that equals one thousandth of a liter. 1 mL = 0.001 L

millimeter A unit of length in the metric system that equals one thousandth of a meter. 1 mm = 0.001 m

misleading A comparing sentence containing language that may trick you into doing the wrong operation.

Example: John's age is 3 *more* than Jessica's. If John is 12, how old is Jessica?

mixed number A number represented by a whole number and a fraction.

Example: $4\frac{2}{3}$

mode The number that appears most frequently in a set of numbers.

Example: 2, 4, 4, 4, 5, 7, 7
4 is the mode in this set of numbers.

Multiplication Column Table A table made of two columns from a multiplication table.

Days	Dollars
0	0
1	3
2	6
3	9
4	12
5	15
6	18
7	21
8	24
9	27

multiplication table A table that shows the product of each pair of numbers in the left column and top row.

multiplier The factor used to multiply the numerator and denominator to create an equivalent fraction.

Example: A multiplier of 5 changes $\frac{2}{3}$ to $\frac{5 \times 2}{5 \times 3} = \frac{10}{15}$.

N

negative number A number less than zero.

Examples: −1, −23, and −3.5 are negative numbers.

net A flat pattern that can be folded to make a solid figure.

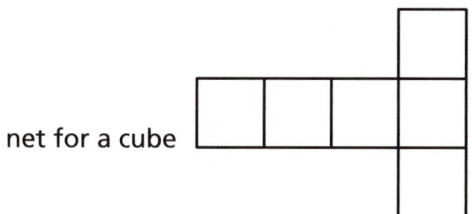

net for a cube

non-unit fraction A fraction with a numerator greater than 1.

Examples: $\frac{3}{4}$ or $\frac{4}{8}$ or $\frac{10}{8}$.

number sentence Describes how numbers or expressions are related to each other using one of the symbols =, <, or >. The types of number sentences are equations and inequalities.

Examples: 25 + 25 = 50
13 > 8 + 2

numerator The number above the bar in a fraction.

Example: The numerator is 2.

$\frac{2}{3}$ ← numerator

It tells how many unit fractions there are: 2 of the $\frac{1}{3}$.

O

oblique lines Lines that are not parallel or perpendicular.

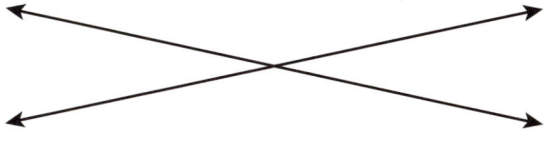

obtuse angle An angle greater than a right angle and less than a straight angle.

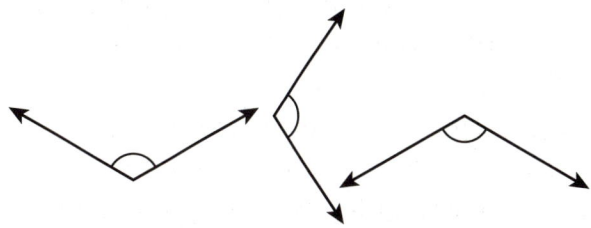

obtuse triangle A triangle with one obtuse angle.

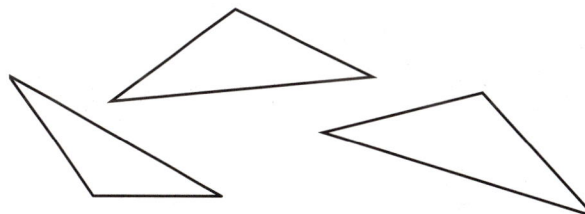

odd number A whole number that is not a multiple of 2. An odd number ends with 1, 3, 5, 7, or 9.

Example: 73 is an odd number because it is not a multiple of 2.

one-dimensional Having only length as a measure. A line segment is one-dimensional.

Order of Operations A set of rules that states the order in which operations should be done.
1. Compute inside parentheses first.
2. Multiply and divide from left to right.
3. Add and subtract from left to right.

ordered pair A pair of numbers that shows the position of a point on a coordinate grid.

Example: The ordered pair (3, 4) represents a point 3 units to the right of the *y*-axis and 4 units above the *x*-axis.

Glossary (Continued)

origin The point (0, 0) on a two-dimensional coordinate grid.

ounce A unit of weight or capacity in the U.S. customary system equal to one sixteenth of a pound or one eighth of a cup.

over-estimate An estimate that is greater than the actual amount.

Example: A shirt costs $26.47 and a pair of jeans cost $37.50. You can make an over-estimate by rounding $26.47 to $30 and $37.50 to $40 to be sure you have enough money to pay for the clothes.

P

parallel The same distance apart at every point.

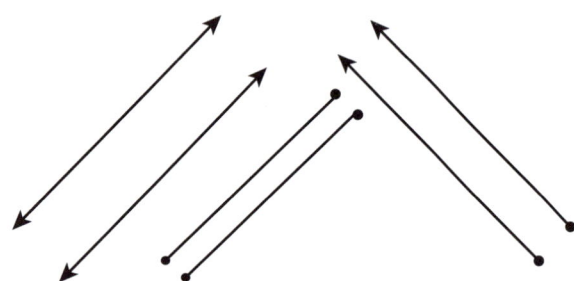

parallelogram A quadrilateral with both pairs of opposite sides parallel.

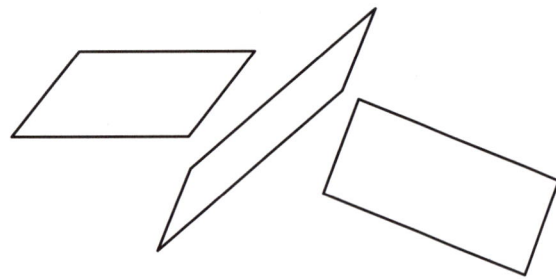

parentheses Symbols used to group numbers together.

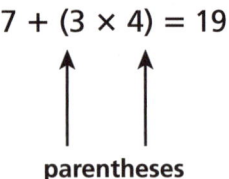

partial products Products of the smaller problems in the Rectangle Sections method of multiplying.

Example: The partial products are highlighted.

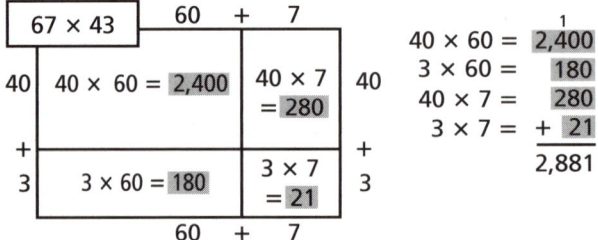

pentagon A polygon with five sides.

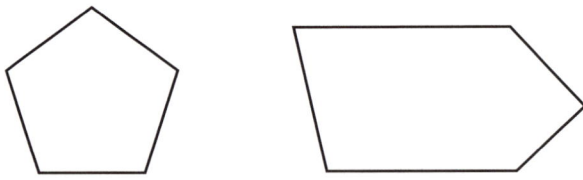

percent Percent means out of a hundred or per hundred. The numerator of a fraction that has 100 as the denominator is followed by the % sign: 50% is 50/100 or a value equivalent to 50/100.

perimeter The distance around a figure.

perpendicular Lines, line segments, or rays are perpendicular if they form right angles.

Example: These two lines are perpendicular.

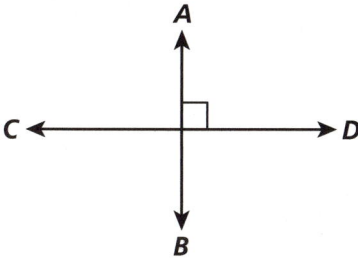

pi A number equal to the circumference of a circle divided by its diameter, or about 3.14. Pi is often represented by the symbol π.

pint A U.S. customary unit of capacity equal to half a quart.

place value The value assigned to the place that a digit occupies in a number.

Example: 235

The 2 is in the hundreds place, so its value is 200.

plane A flat surface that extends without end.

polygon A closed plane figure with sides made of straight line segments.

pound A unit of weight in the U.S. customary system.

prime number A number greater than 1 that has 1 and itself as the only factor pair. Examples of prime numbers are 2, 7, and 13. The only factor pair of 7 is 1 and 7.

prism A solid figure with two congruent parallel bases.

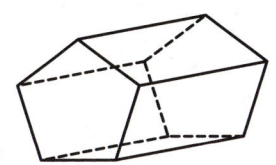

pentagonal prism

probability A number between 0 and 1 that represents the chance of an event happening.

product The result of a multiplication.

Example: 9 × 7 = 63

product

proof A demonstration of the truth of a general statement.

proportion An equation that shows two equivalent ratios.

Example: 6 : 10 = 9 : 15

pyramid A solid with a polygon for a base whose vertices are all joined to a single point.

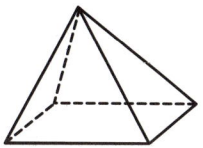

Q

quadrilateral A two-dimensional figure with four sides.

Glossary (Continued)

quart A U.S. customary unit of capacity equal to $\frac{1}{4}$ gallon or 2 pints.

quarter turn A 90° rotation.

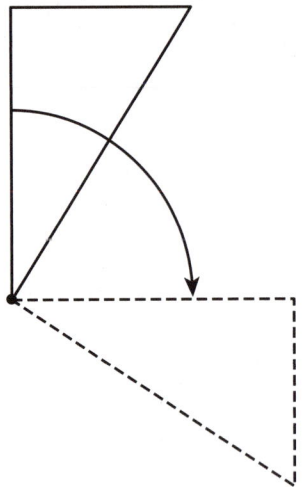

R

radius A line segment that connects the center of a circle to any point on that circle. Also the length of that line segment.

range The greatest number and the least number in a set or the difference between the greatest and the least number in a set.

ratio A comparison of two or more quantities in the same units.

Ratio Table A table that shows equivalent ratios.

Example: This table show ratios equivalent to the basic ratio, 3 : 5.

3	5
0	0
3	5
6	10
9	15
12	20
15	25
18	30
21	35
24	40

ray A part of a line that has one endpoint and extends without end in one direction.

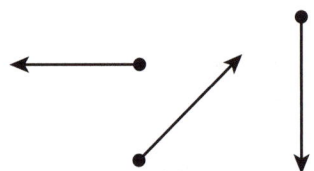

rectangle A parallelogram with four right angles.

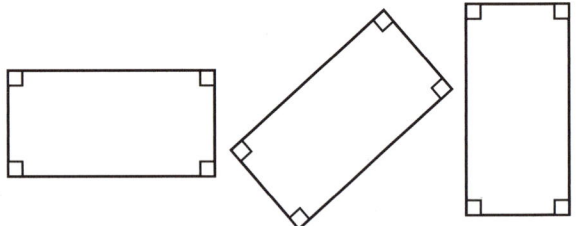

Rectangle Rows A method used to solve multiplication problems.

Example:

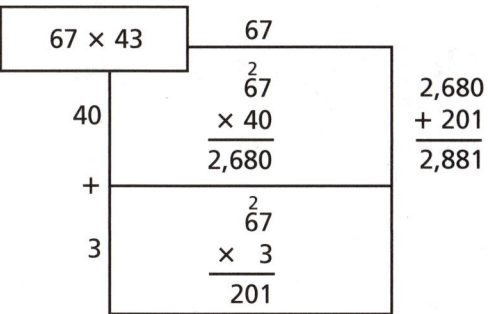

Rectangle Sections A method used to solve multiplication and division problems.

Example:

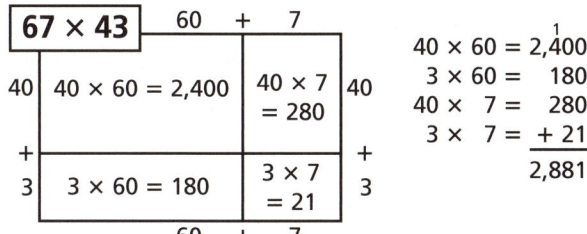

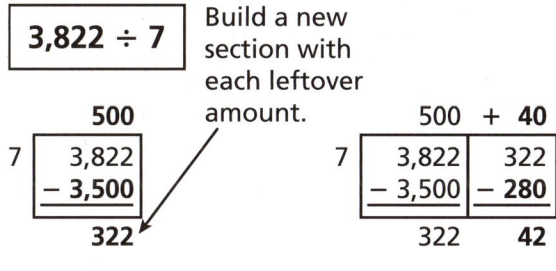

rectangular prism A solid that has congruent rectangular bases.

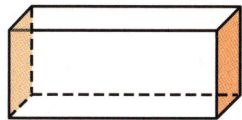

reflection A transformation that flips a figure onto a congruent image. Sometimes called a *flip*.

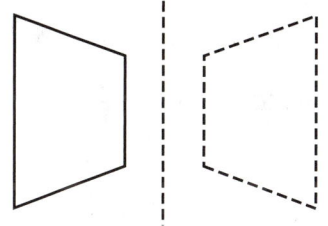

reflex angle An angle greater than 180°.

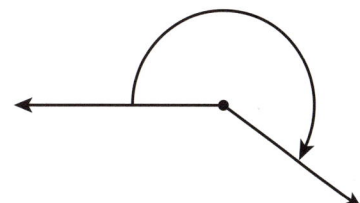

remainder The number left over after dividing a number by a number that does not divide it evenly.

Example: 43 ÷ 5 = 8 R3

The remainder is 3.

Repeated Groups Groups with the same number of objects are Repeated Groups.

Example: 2 + 2 + 2 = 6

There are 3 repeated groups of 2.

rhombus A parallelogram with congruent sides.

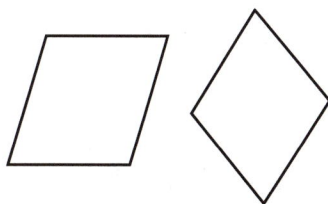

Glossary (Continued)

right angle An angle that measures 90°.

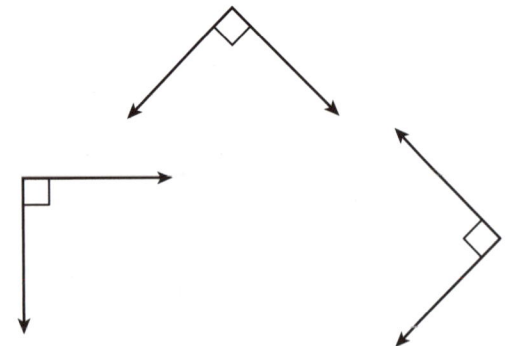

right trapezoid A trapezoid with at least one right angle.

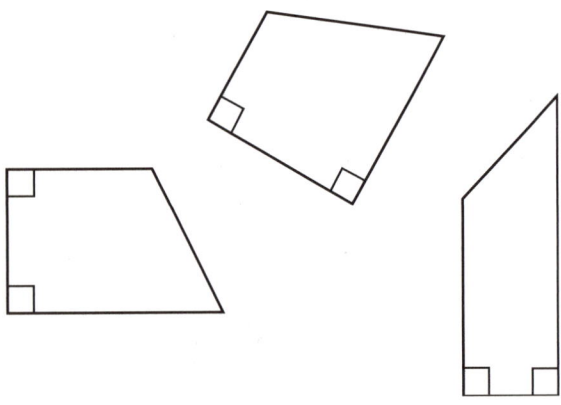

right triangle A triangle with one right angle.

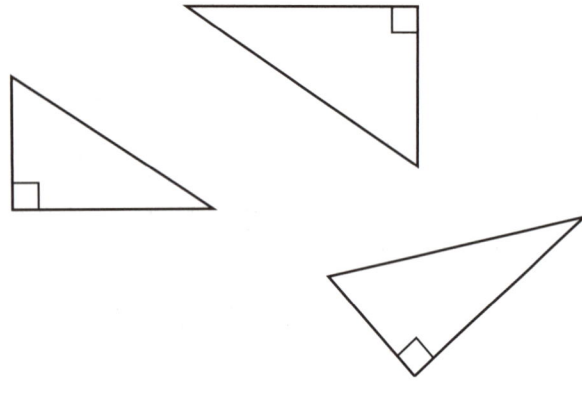

rotation A turn. A transformation that turns a figure so that each point stays an equal distance from a single point, the center of rotation.

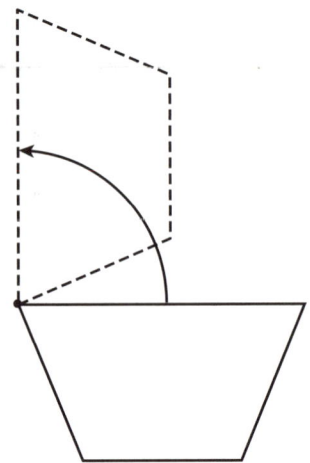

rotational symmetry The property of a figure that allows it to fit exactly on itself in less than one full rotation.

round To find the nearest ten, hundred, thousand, or some other place value.

Example: 463 rounded to the nearest ten is 460.
463 rounded to the nearest hundred is 500.

row A part of a table or array that contains items arranged horizontally.

• • • • •

S

scale Numbers or marks arranged at regular intervals that are used for measurement or to establish position. In a scale drawing, the scale tells how the measurements in the drawing relate to the actual measurements.

scale drawing A drawing that is made in proportion to the size of a real object.

scalene triangle A triangle with no equal sides is a scalene triangle.

Short Cut Method A method used to solve multiplication problems.

Example: 43 × 67

Step 1	Step 2	Step 3	Step 4	Step 5
$\overset{2}{4}3$ × 67 ―― 1	$\overset{2}{4}3$ × 67 ―― 301	$\overset{2}{4}3$ × 67 ―― 301 0	$\overset{\overset{1}{2}}{4}3$ × 67 ―― 301 2,580	$\overset{\overset{1}{2}}{4}3$ × 67 ―― 301 2,580 ―― 2,881

similar Having the same shape but not necessarily the same size. The lengths of the corresponding sides are in proportion.

similar figures

simplest form A fraction is in simplest form if there is no whole number (other than 1) that divides evenly into the numerator and demominator.

Example: $\frac{3}{4}$ This fraction is in simplest form because no number divides evenly into 3 and 4.

simplify To find a result. To rewrite a fraction as an equivalent fraction with a smaller numerator and denominator.

Example: $\frac{3}{6} = \frac{1}{2}$

situation equation An equation that shows the action or the relationship in a problem.

Example: $35 + n = 40$

slant height The height of a triangular face of a pyramid.

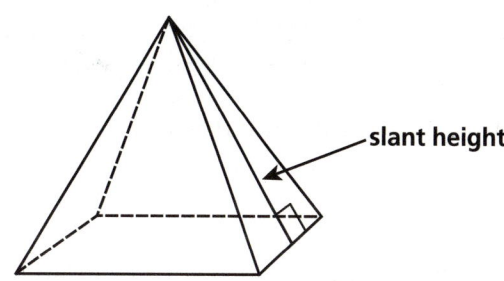

solution equation An equation that shows the operation to perform in order to solve the problem.

Example: $n = 40 - 35$

square A rectangle with four congruent sides.

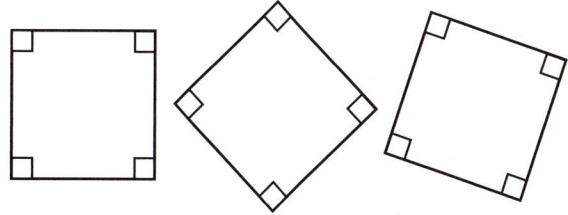

square number The product of a whole number and itself.

Example: $3 \times 3 = 9$
9 is a square number.

square unit A unit of area equal to the area of a square with one-unit sides.

Examples: square meters and square inches

square yard A unit of area equal to the area of a square with one-yard sides.

Glossary (Continued)

standard form The form of a number written using digits.
Example: 2,145

straight angle An angle of 180°.

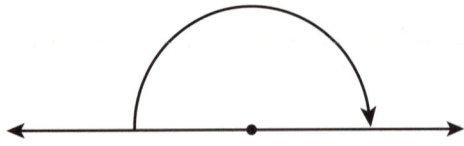

sum The result of an addition.
Example:

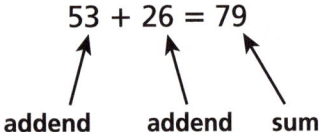

supplementary angles Angles having a sum of 180°.

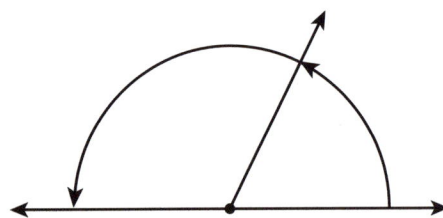

surface area The total area of the two-dimensional surfaces around the outside of a three-dimensional figure.

T

table Data arranged in rows and columns.

three-dimensional Having length measurements in three directions, perpendicular to each other.

ton A unit of weight or mass that equals 2,000 pounds.

tonne A metric unit of mass that equals 1,000 kilograms.

transformation Reflections, rotations, and translations are examples of tranformations.

translation A transformation that moves a figure along a straight line without turning or flipping. Sometimes called a *slide*.

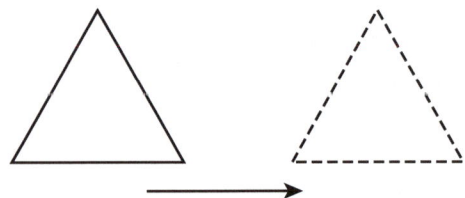

trapezoid A quadrilateral with exactly one pair of parallel sides.

triangle A polygon with three sides.

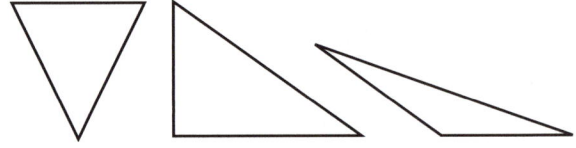

two-dimensional Having length measurements in two directions that are perpendicular to each other.

U

under-estimate An estimate that is less than the actual amount.
Example: A shirt costs $26.47 and a pair of jeans cost $37.50. If you brought $60 to pay for the clothes because you rounded $26.47 to $25 and $37.50 to $35, you made an under-estimate and did not have enough money.

ungroup Rewrite a mixed number with a different whole number and fraction part or rewrite a whole number with different numbers in the places.
Example: $4\frac{2}{3} = 3\frac{5}{3}$ or $100 + 20 + 3 = 90 + 30 + 3$

unit Something used repeatedly to measure quantity.
Examples: Centimeters, pounds, inches, and so on.

unit fraction A fraction with a numerator of 1.
Examples: $\frac{1}{2}$ and $\frac{1}{10}$

unsimplify Rewrite a fraction as an equivalent fraction with a greater numerator and denominator.
Examples: $\frac{1}{2} = \frac{3}{6}$

V

variable A letter or symbol that represents a number.

vertex A point that is shared by two arms of an angle, two sides of a polygon, or edges of a solid figure. The point of a cone.

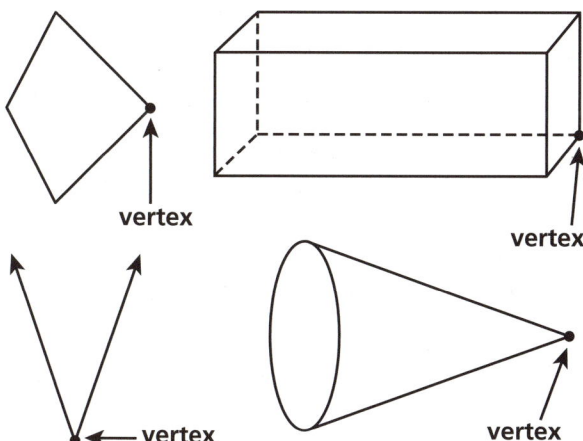

view A two-dimensional representation of what a three-dimensional figure looks like from the front, side, or top.

volume The measure of the amount of space occupied by an object.

W

width The measure of one side or edge of a figure.

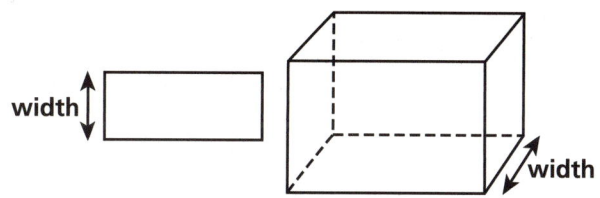

word form The form of a number written using words instead of digits.
Example: Six hundred thirty-nine

X

x-axis The horizontal axis of a two-dimensional coordinate grid.

x-coordinate A number that represents a point's horizontal distance from the y-axis of a two-dimensional coordinate grid.

Y

y-axis The vertical axis of a two-dimensional coordinate grid.

yard A U.S. customary unit of length equal to 3 feet or 36 inches.

y-coordinate A number that represents a point's vertical distance from the x-axis of a two-dimensional coordinate grid.